D1016122

DK Pocket Genius

EARTH

FACTS AT YOUR FINGERTIPS

Penguin Random House

DK DELHI
Project editor Rashmi Rajan
Project art editor Nishesh Batnagar
Senior editor Samira Sood
Senior art editor Govind Mittal
Editor Neha Chaudhary
Art editor Pooja Pipil
DTP designers Jaypal Singh, Arjinder Singh
Picture researcher Sumedha Chopra

DK LONDON
Senior editor Fleur Star
Senior art editor Philip Letsu
US editor Margaret Parrish
Jacket editor Manisha Majithia
Jacket designer Laura Brim
Jacket manager Amanda Lunn
Production editor Adam Stoneham
Production controller Mary Slater
Publisher Andrew Macintyre
Associate publishing director Liz Wheeler
Art director Phil Ormerod
Publishing director Jonathan Metcalf
Consultant Douglas Palmer

TALL TREE LTD.
Editors Rob Colson, Joe Fullman, Jon Richards
Designer Ed Simkins

First American Edition, 2012
This edition published in the United States in 2016 by
DK Publishing, 1450 Broadway, Suite 801, New York, NY 10018

A catalog record for this book
is available from the Library of Congress.
ISBN: 978-1-4654-4586-5

DK books are available at special discounts when
purchased in bulk for sales promotions, premiums,
fund-raising, or educational use. For details, contact:
DK Publishing Special Markets, 1450 Broadway, Suite
801, New York, NY 10018
SpecialSales@dk.com

Printed and bound in China

A WORLD OF IDEAS:
SEE ALL THERE IS TO KNOW

www.dk.com

CONTENTS

Scales and sizes
This book contains profiles of rocks that have scale drawings to indicate size.

6 in
(15 cm)

Levels of clouds
Where the cloud appears is based on the height at which the cloud base occurs.

Troposphere

Locators
A red dot shows the location of a feature and a red rectangle of larger features.

Area locations

Locators
Red shaded areas show the extent of larger features.

Area shading

Formation of the Earth

About 14 billion years ago, the universe was born in an incredibly violent explosion known as the Big Bang. In a fraction of a second the speck-sized universe expanded into a huge fireball of gases. It cooled over time, forming stars, galaxies (large groups of stars), and planets, including the Earth.

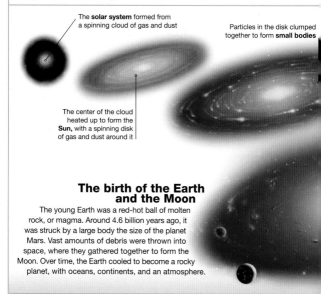

The **solar system** formed from a spinning cloud of gas and dust

Particles in the disk clumped together to form **small bodies**

The center of the cloud heated up to form the **Sun,** with a spinning disk of gas and dust around it

The birth of the Earth and the Moon

The young Earth was a red-hot ball of molten rock, or magma. Around 4.6 billion years ago, it was struck by a large body the size of the planet Mars. Vast amounts of debris were thrown into space, where they gathered together to form the Moon. Over time, the Earth cooled to become a rocky planet, with oceans, continents, and an atmosphere.

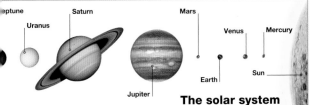

Neptune

Uranus

Saturn

Mars

Venus

Mercury

Jupiter

Earth

Sun

The solar system

The solar system is made up of the Sun, eight planets, more than 170 moons, and millions of small, rocky bodies, such as asteroids and comets. The planets revolve around the Sun in paths called orbits. The four planets closest to the Sun are balls of rock and metal, while the other four are made up mostly of gas and liquid.

The small bodies crashed into each other and joined to create **planets**

Formation of the solar system

GOLDILOCKS PLANET

The Earth is the only planet in our solar system that supports life. It is called a "Goldilocks planet," after the story of *Goldilocks and the Three Bears*. Just as Goldilocks found the porridge that was "just right" for her to eat, the Earth is "just right" to support life—neither too hot nor too cold, and with large amounts of liquid water, which allows life to flourish.

Geological timeline

People who study the Earth are called geologists. Using sources such as fossils, rocks, and minerals, they have divided the Earth's history into different portions of time. The longest are called eons, which are made up of eras, which consist of periods.

First life

About three billion years ago, the first traces of life appeared in the form of bacteria living in shallow seas. They built mounds out of sand, called stromatolites. These mounds are still forming in some areas today, and provide a record of life on the Earth.

Stromatolites

PERIOD	Cambrian	Ordovician	Silurian	Devonian	Carbonife
ERA	542 million years ago (mya)		PALEOZOIC ERA		
EON	PHANEROZOIC				

Complex life

Life-forms grew much more complex during the Cambrian period. From Ordovician times onward, small land plants began to develop. By the Devonian period, bigger fernlike and treelike plants formed the first forests, along with giant fungi, such as *Prototaxites*. These provided habitats for the first land animals.

About 7 in (18 cm) Aglaophyton are dwarfed by giant fungi

Coelophysis

The origin of humans

Many modern mammals, including horses, camels, and cows, first appeared in the Neogene Period. Hominids—the ancestors of humans—appeared in Africa and spread across the world. *Homo habilis* was a hominid that lived in East Africa about two million years ago.

Age of dinosaurs

Dinosaurs first evolved in the Triassic Period as small, two-legged animals, such as *Coelophysis*. They continued to evolve in the Jurassic Period, and became the dominant life-forms on land.

Homo habilis

...nian	Triassic	Jurassic	Cretaceous	Paleogene	Neogene
	▶ 252 mya	**MESOZOIC ERA**		▶ 65 mya	**CENOZOIC ERA**

Mass extinction

Fossil records show that at the end of the Cretaceous Period, about 65 million years ago, an asteroid or comet collided with the Earth. It is thought to have killed huge numbers of species, including the dinosaurs. This marked the end of the Mesozoic Era.

Inside the Earth

The inside of the Earth has three main layers: a thin, cool outer crust; a thick, hot mantle; and an even hotter metallic core. The movement of heat from the core through the mantle has caused the rocks of the Earth's crust to change over time.

The Earth **bulges** at the equator

Inner core is 1,700 miles (2,740 km) thick

Direction of the **Earth's rotation**

Shape and form
The force of gravity pulls the Earth into an almost perfect sphere. However, the Earth rotates on its axis, which causes it to bulge slightly at the equator.

The Earth's layers
The Earth's outermost layer is the crust, which is made of soil and rock. Under this is the mantle, where liquid rock, or magma, flows in huge swirls. However, the inside, or core, of the Earth has two sections—an outer core of thick liquid rock, and a solid inner core.

Layers of the Earth

er core is 1,240 miles
0 km) thick

Mantle is 1,800 miles
(2,900 km) thick

TYPES OF ROCK

Igneous rocks form from molten rock that has cooled and turned solid. They originate from deep inside the Earth, and may form at or below the Earth's surface.

Sedimentary rocks form at the Earth's surface and are made up of clearly visible layers of minerals, rock pieces, or organic matter (such as the remains of animals and plants).

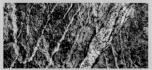

Metamorphic rocks, such as this quartzite rock, form when existing rocks are squeezed by pressure and heated deep under the Earth's crust.

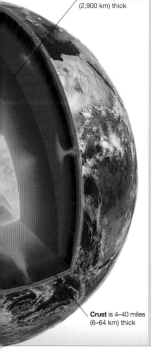

Crust is 4–40 miles
(6–64 km) thick

The moving Earth

The Earth's crust is broken up into huge, irregularly shaped pieces called tectonic plates. These plates are pushed around by the movement of magma in the mantle below. This movement causes th Earth to change gradually, over millions of years—continents have be created, oceans have opened and closed, and mountains have risen

Plate tectonics

More than 200 million years ago, the Earth consisted of one large landmass—a "supercont called Pangaea. The movement of the Earth's tectonic plates over millions of years broke this landmass, creating the modern continents. This movement of plates is known as pla tectonics, and continues to take place today.

270 million years ago

200 million years ago

Today

The Earth's plates

There are 30 tectonic plates, of which seven cover 94 percent of the Earth. The rest is made up of 23 smaller plates. The boundaries, or edges, of tectonic plates are usually marked by mountains, earthquake and volcanic zones, and oceanic trenches.

The Earth's tectonic plates

ate boundary

ere two tectonic plates meet,
erent types of plate boundary are
ned, based on how the plates move.
te movement can cause earthquakes
d volcanic eruptions.

Where plates crash
into each other, a
convergent boundary
occurs. Here, one plate
may be pushed beneath
the other in a process
called subduction.

A **divergent boundary**
is created where plates
move away from each
other. Molten lava may
rise up from the mantle
to fill the gap at this
type of boundary.

Where two plates
scrape past each
other, a **transform
boundary** occurs.

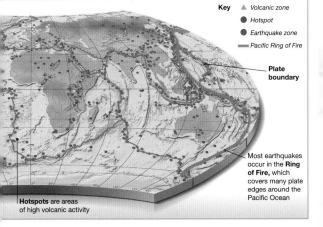

Key
- ▲ Volcanic zone
- ● Hotspot
- ● Earthquake zone
- ▬ Pacific Ring of Fire

Plate
boundary

Most earthquakes
occur in the **Ring
of Fire,** which
covers many plate
edges around the
Pacific Ocean

Hotspots are areas
of high volcanic activity

Fault systems

The constant movement of the Earth's tectonic plates causes its crust to split apart. This can lead to massive blocks of rock slipping past one another, resulting in huge cracks in the Earth's surface called faults. Plates sometimes get stuck as they push past each other, causing energy to build up. When they eventually slip free, the sudden jolt can cause an earthquake.

San Andreas Fault

The San Andreas Fault slices across California's coastal region. To its west is the Pacific plate, which stretches from the edge of California almost to Asia. To the east is the North American plate, which makes up most of the continent. The inhabited areas on this fault, particularly in southern California, are prone to earthquakes.

LOCATION From Cape Mendocino, northern California, to the Gulf of California

PLATE BOUNDARY TYPE Transform

LENGTH 808 miles (1,300 km)

Over the last century, the San Andreas Fault has been moving at an average rate of 2 in (5 cm) every year.

[Gr]eat Rift Valley

[Afri]ca's Great Rift Valley runs through [the] middle of Kenya. It is part of a huge set of [cra]cks in the Earth's crust called the East African [Rift] System. In northeastern Africa, this system [divi]des the African plate from the Arabian plate, [split]ting past the Sinai Peninsula.

[LO]CATION From the southern Red Sea, [thro]ugh East Africa, to Beira in Mozambique

[PL]ATE BOUNDARY TYPE Divergent

[LE]NGTH 4,000 miles (6,400 km)

Sinai Peninsula

Sunda Megathrust

This fault lay inactive for a thousand years. But in 2004, a part of it slipped, causing a huge earthquake and tsunami in the Indian Ocean. Giant waves swept far inland, destroying coastlines and killing about 280,000 people.

LOCATION From Bangladesh, through Sumatra, Bali, and Indonesia, to northwestern Australia

PLATE BOUNDARY TYPE Convergent

LENGTH 3,400 miles (5,500 km)

Great Alpine Fault

About 26 million years ago, the movement of the Pacific and Australian plates formed the Great Alpine Fault. Plate movement pushed the land up, creating the Southern Alps.

LOCATION New Zealand's South Island west coast from Fiordland to Blenheim

PLATE BOUNDARY TYPE Transform

LENGTH 310 miles (500 km)

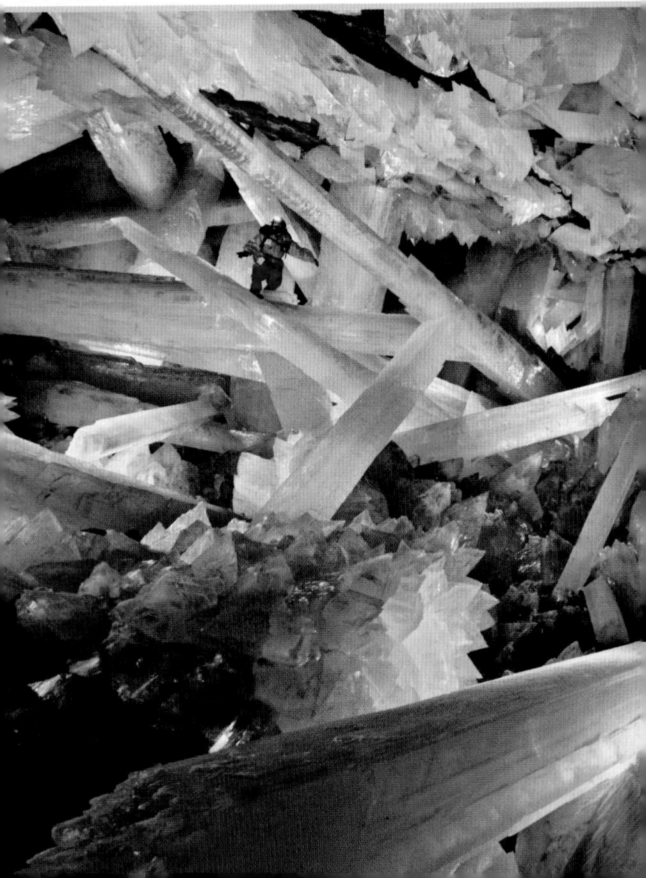

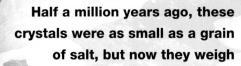

Half a million years ago, these crystals were as small as a grain of salt, but now they weigh

55 tons

CAVE OF CRYSTALS

Giant crystals of selenite, a form of the mineral gypsum, are found 1,000 ft (300 m) below the Naica mine in Mexico. They formed when a magma chamber boiled the water below the Earth's surface at a consistent temperature for 500,000 years. The heat solidified the crystals in the water and helped them grow. They are now some of the largest natural crystals in the world.

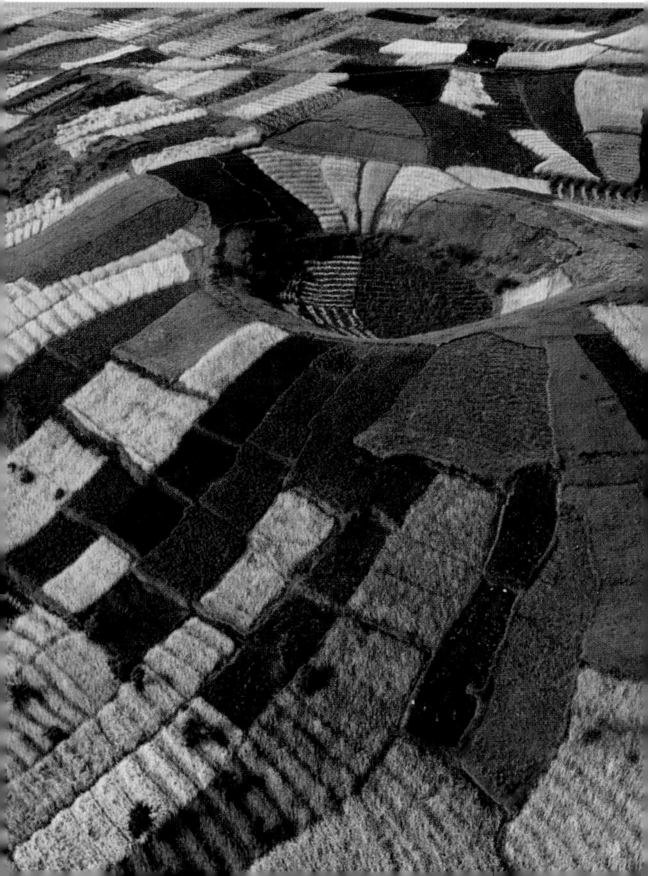

Land

About 30 percent of the Earth's surface is covered by land. A wide range of landscapes are found on the Earth, including mountains, deserts, forests, and grasslands. Many of these landscapes are shaped by the wind and rain, while others, such as deltas and valleys, are formed by rivers and glaciers. Human activity can also shape the landscape. People use the countryside as farmland to grow crops or herd animals, while urban areas feature tall buildings and well-developed roads and highways.

VOLCANIC EFFECT
Volcanic eruptions can change the landscape in many ways. When lava comes into contact with water, it can cool to form islands. Also, volcanic ash acts as fertilizer, helping plants grow.

World biomes

Regions that share the same climate, soils, vegetation, and animals are known as biomes. Scientists divide the world into a number of biomes, or habitats, ranging from dry deserts with very little life to wet rainforests teeming with plants and animals.

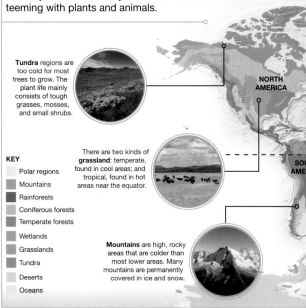

Tundra regions are too cold for most trees to grow. The plant life mainly consists of tough grasses, mosses, and small shrubs.

NORTH AMERICA

There are two kinds of **grassland**: temperate, found in cool areas; and tropical, found in hot areas near the equator.

SOU AME

KEY

- Polar regions
- Mountains
- Rainforests
- Coniferous forests
- Temperate forests
- Wetlands
- Grasslands
- Tundra
- Deserts
- Oceans

Mountains are high, rocky areas that are colder than most lower areas. Many mountains are permanently covered in ice and snow.

Wetlands are waterlogged or flooded areas of land. They may have salty or fresh water, and include mangroves, bogs, marshes, and fens.

Antarctica and the Arctic form the **polar regions,** which are the Earth's coldest zones. Polar regions cover about 20 percent of the Earth's surface.

EUROPE

ASIA

AFRICA

Coniferous forests form the world's largest continuous land biome. They consist of coniferous trees that cover about 17 percent of the Earth's land area.

EQUATOR

The largest biome on the Earth, **oceans** support a huge range of living species, from tiny plankton to the biggest animal in the world—the blue whale.

AUSTRALIA

Temperate forests lie roughly midway between the poles and the equator. They have distinct warm and cold seasons called summer and winter.

Rainforests are found in regions with very wet climates. Tropical rainforests contain more plant and animal life than any other biome on the Earth.

...erts cover about ...fth of the Earth's ...urface. They receive ...or no rain and very ...nimals and plants ...n them.

ANTARCTICA

Mountains

Masses of rock that rise high above their surroundings are called mountains. They are pushed up by plate movements over many millions of years to create soaring peaks. At present, mountains cover 20 percent of the Earth's land surface.

FOCUS ON...
LIFE

Many plants and animals have adapted to the cold temperatures of the mountains.

▲ Lady Amherst's pheasant lives in the mountain forests of Asia. It moves up and down the mountains with the seasons.

▲ The dark color of the Bhutan glory helps it to absorb sunlight and warm up quickly in the cold.

▲ The small, tough leaves of alpine plants reduce water loss and protect them from very cold temperatures.

Rocky Mountains

The Rocky Mountains are made up of at least 100 separate ranges. They are part of one of the largest mountain belts on Earth—the Western Cordillera. The landscape of the mountain chain is complex and varied, with towering peaks and active volcanoes.

LOCATION Western North America, from Alaska to New Mexico
HIGHEST PEAK Mount Elbert, Colorado (14,431 ft/4,399 m
LENGTH 3,000 miles (4,800 km)

...des

Andes is the longest mountain chain in the ...d. Its peaks rise suddenly from sea level on ...Pacific coast of South America to altitudes ...ver 21,500 ft (6,500 m). It is one of the ...h's most active mountain belts. There ...requent earthquakes as well as ...tions from 183 active volcanoes.

Mount Fitzroy in Patagonia, southern Andes

...CATION Down western ...th America, from the ...bbean Sea to Cape Horn

...HEST PEAK ...ncagua, Argentina ...335 ft/6,960 m)

...GTH ...0 miles (7,200 km)

...als

... known as "the stone belt," the Ural ...untain range separates Europe from Asia. ...central and southern parts of this range ...covered with thick forests, while farther ...n, there are alpine meadows and tundra.

LOCATION From the Arctic Ocean to the border between Russia and Kazakhstan

HIGHEST PEAK Narodnaya, Russia (6,215 ft/1,895 m)

LENGTH 1,500 miles (2,400 km)

Pyrenees

During the Cretaceous Period, Iberia split from the supercontinent of Pangaea. As the Atlantic Ocean opened, the Iberian plate was squeezed between Europe and North Africa, forming the Pyrenees. This range has some of Europe's most spectacular waterfalls and many limestone caves with paintings by early modern humans.

LOCATION Between France and Spain, from the Atlantic Ocean to the Mediterranean Sea
HIGHEST PEAK Aneto, Spain (11,170 ft/3,405 m)
LENGTH 270 miles (435 km)

Alps

The Alps were created when the African and Eurasian plates collided around 90 million years ago. These mountains form a curved belt, with many peaks rising to above 13,000 ft (4,000 m). They form the largest mountain range in Europe.

Atlas Mountains

These mountains do not form a continuous chain, but a series of different ranges. The northern ranges get plenty of rainfall and feature cedar, pine, and oak forests. The southern ranges are drier and have salt flats in areas close to the Sahara.

CATION Across southern Europe,
m Mediterranean France to Austria

HIGHEST PEAK Mont Blanc, France
(15,770 ft/4,805 m)

LENGTH 650 miles (1,050 km)

Drakensberg Plateau

Although the Drakensberg Plateau is
made up of sedimentary rocks, it is covered with
a layer of basalt, an igneous rock. This layer was
originally 4,900 ft (1,500 m) thick and covered an
area of about 800,000 sq miles (2 million sq km),
but over time, much has been worn away. The
plateau has steep sandstone cliffs, individual
pinnacles, waterfalls, and huge caves.

LOCATION From northeastern to southern
South Africa, through Swaziland and Lesotho

HIGHEST PEAK Ntlenyana, Lesotho
(11,417 ft/3,480 m)

LENGTH 800 miles (1,290 km)

CATION From the Atlantic coast
Morocco to the Mediterranean east
ast of Tunisia

GHEST PEAK Toubkal, Morocco
,665 ft/4,165 m)

NGTH 1,500 miles (2,400 km)

Himalayas

Formed within the last 50 million years, the Himalayas are one of the world's youngest mountain belts. They are the highest mountains on the Earth, and are getting higher at a rate of $\frac{1}{6}$ in (4 mm) every year, because the Indian plate is still pushing into the Eurasian plate.

LOCATION From northern Pakistan and India, across Nepal and Bhutan to China

HIGHEST PEAK Mount Everest, Nepal (29,035 ft/8,850 m)

LENGTH 1,500 miles (2,400 km)

Great Dividing Range

This range is one of Australia's most important geographical features, since it is the source of many of the country's major rivers, including the Murray and the Darling. It runs along the length of Australia's eastern coast, with the highest peaks in the south.

LOCATION From the Cape York Peninsula, Queensland, along Australia's eastern coast to Tasmania

HIGHEST PEAK Mount Kosciuszko, Australia (7,310 ft/2,230 m)

LENGTH 2,237 miles (3,600 km)

uthern Alps

w Zealand's Alps were formed by the
lision of the Pacific plate and the Australian
e. The range is at its highest near the center.
western slopes are covered in forests because
he year-round rains brought by the winds
wing from that direction.

LOCATION New Zealand's South
Island, from northeast to southwest

HIGHEST PEAK Mount Cook, New Zealand
(12,285 ft/3,745 m)

LENGTH 300 miles (500 km)

nsantarctic Mountains

The curved belt of the Transantarctic
Mountains separates the higher region of
Greater Antarctica in the east from the lower
Lesser Antarctica in the west. This belt includes
many volcanoes, some of which are still active,
such as Deception Island.

LOCATION Across Antarctica, from
Oates Land to the Antarctic Peninsula

HIGHEST PEAK Mount Kirkpatrick, Antarctica
(14,856 ft/4,528 m)

LENGTH 2,200 miles (3,500 km)

Volcanoes

A volcano is both an opening in the Earth's crust through which magma, ash, and hot gases erupt from below its surface, and the structure created by this eruption. Volcanic eruptions can cause widespread destruction.

FOCUS ON...
TYPES
There are many different types of volcano, depending on their shape or the way they were form

Crater Lake

About 7,000 years ago, a massive eruption destroyed Mount Mazama and formed a crater, or caldera. Over time, heavy rain and snowfall caused water levels in the crater to rise, creating Crater Lake. As the lake is not fed by streams or rivers, which carry sediments—particles of rock, mineral, or plant and animal remains—its water is extremely clear.

LOCATION Southern Cascade Range, Oregon

TYPE Collapsed stratovolcano

HEIGHT 8,170 ft (2,490 m)

Kilauea

Kilauea is the most active of the overlapping volcanoes that have built up the island of Haw which rises more than 13,000 ft (4,000 m) from ocean floor. Since 1983, flows from Kilauea ha covered more than 40 sq miles (100 sq km).

LOCATION Southeast Hawaii

TYPE Shield volcano

HEIGHT 4,000 ft (1,220 m)

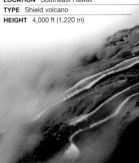

A stratovolcano is cone-shaped, with steep slopes. Is built of many layers of lava and ash.

▲ A shield volcano is formed when runny basalt lava flows across the ground. It is usually broad, with shallow slopes.

▲ A submarine volcano forms deep under water and its eruption may or may not reach sea level.

Surtsey

In November 1963, a series of volcanic explosions occurred off the coast of southern Iceland. When the smoke cleared, a new island had appeared above the waves. The Icelandic government named it Surtsey, after Surtur, a mythical Norse fire giant. The island continued to emit clouds of ash and fountains of lava until 1967, when it finally fell quiet.

LOCATION	Off the coast of Iceland
TYPE	Submarine
HEIGHT	500 ft (150 m) above sea level

Mount Etna

Europe's highest active volcano, Etna is almost constantly erupting. It produces rivers of basaltic lava that flow down to the foot of the volcano on all sides.

LOCATION	Eastern Sicily, southwest Italy
TYPE	Stratovolcano
HEIGHT	10,990 ft (3,350 m)

Mount Kilimanjaro

Rising from the savanna plains of eastern Africa, Kilimanjaro is the highest mountain on the continent. It is made up of three volcanic cones—Kibo, Mawenzi, and Shira—of which the central snow-capped cone, Kibo, is the highest.

LOCATION Southern end of the
Great Rift Valley, northeastern Tanzania

TYPE Stratovolcano

HEIGHT 19,340 ft (5,895 m)

Mount Fuji

Japan's highest mountain, Mount Fuji
began to grow over 11,000 years ago on top
of the remains of an older volcano. Within just
3,000 years, lava pouring out of its crater had
built up 80 percent of its present mass.

LOCATION Honshu Island, southwest Tokyo

TYPE Stratovolcano

HEIGHT 12,390 ft (3,775 m)

Mount Erebus

Glacier-covered Erebus is the
southernmost active volcano on the Earth, and
is one of three major volcanoes on Antarctica's
Ross Island. Unusually, the crater at the top of
Mount Erebus is permanently filled with
molten lava.

LOCATION Ross Island, off the Scott Coast

TYPE Stratovolcano

HEIGHT 12,450 ft (3,795 m)

In 1991, the eruption
of Mount Pinatubo

lowered the Earth's temperatures

by 1°F (0.5°C) for a year

VOLCANIC ASH CLOUD
Dust and ash can rain down for days after a volcanic eruption. The ash enters the atmosphere and blocks sunlight, affecting the weather. The 1991 eruption of Mount Pinatubo, in the Philippines, covered the surrounding region in a thick layer of ash.

Volcanic features

When magma cools and solidifies under the Earth's surface, it creates a variety of features in different ways. Some are formed from igneous rock, some from water heated up by magma, and others from collapsed craters.

FOCUS ON...
LAVA
Magma that has erupted onto the Earth's surface is ca lava. It can take var forms after it cools.

Yellowstone Caldera

This huge volcanic caldera is 45 miles (72 km) wide. It contains about 200 geysers—springs that release bursts of hot water and steam. It also has thousands of fumaroles (volcanic outlets that emit steam and other gases), boiling mud pools, and hot springs producing a steady stream of hot water.

LOCATION Yellowstone National Park, Wyoming

TYPE Geyser, hot spring, and fumarole

AGE 600,000 years

Pahoehoe is a fast and both flowing hot lava. On cooling, it forms a wrinkled, skinlike skin.

▲ Aa is a basaltic lava that is thicker, stickier, and slower-flowing than pahoehoe. It forms a rough surface when it cools.

▲ Pillow lava is a pillow-shaped rock formed when lava erupts under water or comes in contact with water.

Devil's Tower

Devil's Tower is a volcanic plug—a core of solidified magma blocking the neck of a volcano. Over millions of years, the surrounding sedimentary rocks wore away, leaving behind a tall, towerlike structure of igneous rock.

LOCATION Great Plains of Wyoming

TYPE Plug

AGE 40 million years

Valley of Ten Thousand Smokes

In 1912, Novarupta Volcano erupted, filling the Ukak valley with ash. The water below the volcanic material heated up and worked its way up to the surface. For the next 15 years, snakelike wisps of steam escaped through thousands of cracks, which gave this valley its name.

LOCATION Alaskan Peninsula

TYPE Fumarole

AGE 100 years

El Capitan and Half Dome

Batholiths are huge masses of igneous rock, which often form the core of mountains. Yosemite Valley, in the Sierra Nevada batholith, features huge, steep vertical cliffs and walls of granite. El Capitan, Yosemite's highest rock wall, rises more than 3,000 ft (900 m) above the valley floor. The area's steepest wall, Half Dome, was formed when a large glacier eroded away one side of the dome.

LOCATION Yosemite National Park, Sierra Nevada, California

TYPE Batholith

AGE 82 million years

Giant's Causeway

This vent was formed as a result of intense volcanic activity about 60 million years ago. The eruption threw out large quantities of liquid basalt lava, which cooled to form about 40,000 hexagonal columns along the sea coast.

LOCATION Northernmost point of County Antrim, Northern Ireland, UK

TYPE Fissure vent

AGE 50–60 million years

Aïr Mountains

The Aïr Mountains were created by volcanic eruptions after three continental plates collided. They are made up of ring dikes—circular sets of igneous intrusions formed around a volcano. Each set of rings is about 40 miles (60 km) in diameter, and contains dikes up to 650 ft (200 m) thick.

LOCATION	Northern parts of Niger, Africa, within the southern Sahara Desert
TYPE	Ring dike
AGE	410 million years

...hin Sill

... igneous intrusion is created when ...gma enters cracks in existing rock. Often, ...ools into a flat layer called a sill. Whin Sill ... a collection of such sills, formed when ...gma rose from beneath the Earth's crust ...d spread. The name "whin" is a local word ...r hard, black stone.

...CATION	Northern Pennine hills, England
...PE	Sill
...E	295 million years

Rocks

Rocks are solid materials—consisting of one or more minerals—that make up the Earth's crust. Based on how they are formed, rocks can be classified into three main types—igneous, which form when magma becomes solid; sedimentary, which form when rock pieces or organic matter get deposited; and metamorphic, which form when there is a change in temperature or pressure.

Granite

This rock is formed when magma cools slowly deep in the Earth's crust. Its toughness and resistance to erosion (wearing away) make it a popular choice for constructing roads and buildings.

TYPE Igneous

FORMATION Intense heat

MINERALS Potassium-feldspar, quartz, sodium, and mica

COLOR White-red, pale green-blue, and gray-black

Basalt

The most common volcanic igneous rock on the Earth's surface, basalt forms the rock floor of most of the world's oceans. It is also found in large amounts on the Moon.

TYPE Igneous

FORMATION Intense heat

MINERALS Sodium plagioclase, pyroxene, and olivine

COLOR Grayish black to black when fresh

ist

ist originates deep within mountain
ges. It usually has a medium to coarse
texture, with visible
mineral grains. It is rich
in minerals such as
mica and quartz.

E Metamorphic

MATION High pressure and temperature

ERALS Quartz, mica, and feldspar

OR Variable, including white and shades
ray, green, blue, brown, and black

Slate

Slate is mud that has been heavily
compressed, or packed together by
pressure. Because of this
compression, it is hard
and waterproof, and
can be split into thin
sheets—all of which
make it ideal for
covering roofs.

TYPE Metamorphic

FORMATION Pressure

MINERALS Quartz, mica, and feldspar

COLOR Gray, also tinged green or purple

rble

Marble is valued for its
smooth texture and color.
It is easy to use in sculpture and
construction. Pure marble is white,
but some types have colorful
patterns due to the presence of
various minerals in them.

TYPE Metamorphic

FORMATION Heat and pressure

MINERALS Calcite

COLOR Mainly white, pink, green,
brown, and black

Limestone

This rock is made of the mineral calcite, which comes from sea water or the shells and skeletons of sea animals. On burning, it reduces lime, a mineral that is used to make cement.

TYPE Sedimentary

FORMATION Surface water deposition

MINERALS Calcite

COLOR Variable, but mostly white or pale shades of yellow, gray, or brown

Sandstone

Sandstones are common rocks formed by deposits from air or water. Different types of sandstone form when minerals or rock grains the size of sand particles get stuck together. Sandstones are classified based on their texture.

TYPE Sedimentary

FORMATION
Surface deposition

MINERALS Quartz and feldspar

COLOR Variable, including white, yellow, brown, to red-black

Conglomerate

When larger rock debris is pressed together, it forms conglomerates. These may be made up of small pebbles, medium-sized cobbles, or large boulders. These rocks rarely contain fossils, because of their coarse nature and the tough conditions in which they are formed.

TYPE Sedimentary

FORMATION Surface water compression

MINERALS Calcite

COLOR Mainly white, pink, green, brown, and black

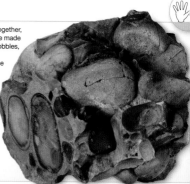

Coal

This organic rock is made from the compressed remains of plants that existed millions of years ago. An important source of energy, coal is used to heat homes and generate electricity.

TYPE Sedimentary

FORMATION Compressed plant debris

MINERALS Clay

COLOR Black

Evaporites

When hot, mineral-rich, salty water evaporates, it leaves behind minerals, such as halite (rock salt) and gypsum. Rocks made of these minerals are called evaporites. The crystal-like texture of these rocks is caused by the formation of salt crystals during evaporation. Many evaporites are used in the production of fertilizers and explosives.

TYPE Sedimentary

FORMATION Surface evaporation of salty water

MINERALS Halite and gypsum

COLOR Usually white or pale shades of yellow and gray, through to red

Crystal-like structure

Rivers

A river is a channel of water that flows toward an ocean, lake, or sea. Smaller streams of water that flow into a river are known as its tributaries. Rivers are a powerful erosive force and they can wear down mountains, carve out valleys, and create wide flood plains.

Mississippi

Along with its tributaries, the Mississippi forms a huge river system, which covers almost all of the US. Levees, or floodbanks, have been built along this river for protection against floods.

LOCATION US, from Canadian border in Minnesota to Gulf of Mexico

LENGTH 2,350 miles (3,780 km)

TRIBUTARIES Missouri, Ohio, Arkansas, and Tennessee

Amazon

...erms of both the size of its basin (hollow ...pression) and the volume of water it carries, ...Amazon is the largest river on the Earth. Its ...w-moving stretches are covered with plants, ...ch as giant water lilies, the leaves of which ...grow up to about 6½ ft (2 m) wide.

LOCATION Peruvian Andes, across Brazil to the Atlantic Ocean

LENGTH 3,995 miles (6,430 km)

TRIBUTARIES Jurua, Madeira, and Negro

Thames

...e Thames originates from springs ...he Cotswolds, a ridge of limestone hills. ...e longest river entirely in England, it flows ...ugh a wide valley with clay deposits.

LOCATION Britain, across southern England ...m the Cotswold Hills to the North Sea

LENGTH 210 miles (335 km)

TRIBUTARIES Colne, Kennet, and Wey

Danube

The Danube begins at the meeting point of the Brege and Brigach rivers. The river also features the Iron Gate—the deepest gorge in Europe, with sides 2,625 ft (800 m) high.

LOCATION Southern Germany to the Black Sea coast in eastern Romania

LENGTH 1,780 miles (2,860 km)

TRIBUTARIES Drava, Sava, and Tisza

Nile

The Nile is the longest river in the world. It is a valuable source of water for the region and has produced rich farmland along its banks. In the winter, rains and snowmelt from the Ethiopian mountains would cause the Nile to flood, depositing fertile soil across the flood plain. However, the construction of the Aswan High Dam in 1970 controlled this annual flooding and farmers now have to use artificial fertilizers.

LOCATION	From Lake Victoria and the Ethiopian Highlands through to the Mediterranean coast
LENGTH	4,130 miles (6,650 km)
TRIBUTARIES	White Nile, Blue Nile, and Atbara

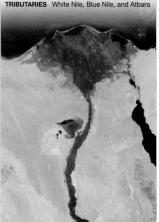

Congo

The Congo is an important source of food and transportation to the people who live along its banks, but they live with the risk of flooding. Its flow is so strong and constant that it does not fo a delta (a deposition of sediments at a river's mouth). Instead, it flows far out into the Atlantic Ocean, depositing sediments on the ocean floo

Indus

Like the Nile, the Indus was one of the rivers alongside which the first civilizations were founded. This river floods frequently in the summer, which can be dangerous for people who live along its banks.

CATION From east Africa, across
continent to the Atlantic Ocean

NGTH 2,900 miles (4,670 km)

BUTARIES Kwa, Lualaba, Sangha,
Ubangi

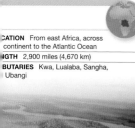

Ganges

One of the most sacred rivers in India,
the Ganges is worshiped as a goddess by
Hindus. It carries more sand and silt to the
sea than any other river in the world.

LOCATION Along the Himalayas to the
Bay of Bengal in India

LENGTH 1,555 miles (2,505 km)

TRIBUTARIES Brahmaputra, Ghaghar,
and Yamuna

CATION Tibetan Plateau, across
Himalayas to the Arabian Sea

NGTH 1,800 miles (2,900 km)

BUTARIES Chenab, Kabul, Jhelum,
Sutlej

Murray

The water of the Murray is so salty
that it cannot be used for anything
except irrigation and power generation.

LOCATION Australia, from the Great Dividing
Range to the Indian Ocean

LENGTH 1,610 miles (2,590 km)

TRIBUTARIES Darling and Murrumbidgee

In 1931, the Yangtze River flooded the cities of Nanjing and Wuhan, killing about 300,000 people and leaving

40 million homeless

THE WALLED RIVER
In the last 2,000 years, the Yangtze River in China has flooded at least 100 times, causing major destruction. To protect the surrounding areas from flooding, the banks of the Yangtze have been raised and dams have been built along its length.

River features

As a river flows, it carves through the landscape or deposits sediments, creating various features along the way, such as waterfalls and deltas. Rivers can also dissolve rocks, creating karst landscapes with underground caves and passages.

Carlsbad Cavern

Inside Carlsbad Caverns National Park, there are 110 limestone caves, including Carlsbad. This cavern has huge stalactites and stalagmites made of calcium and other minerals. The Big Room, formed about four million years ago, is its largest chamber, with an area of 357,480 sq ft (33,210 sq m).

LOCATION Guadalupe Mountains of southern New Mexico

TYPE Underground cave

RIVER Pecos

Niagara Falls

The Niagara Falls are the second largest waterfall in the world, and include the Bridal Veil, American, and Horseshoe falls. Originally, $5\frac{1}{2}$ billion gallons (20 billion liters) of water flowed over the falls every hour. Today, dams and tunnels have been built to control the flow.

LOCATION Border between Canada and US

TYPE Waterfall

RIVER Niagara

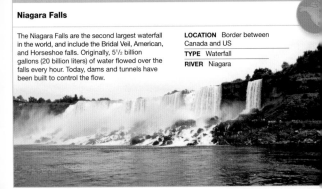

Vercors

Covering about 400 sq miles (1,000 sq km), Vercors is the largest karst area in Europe. It has many long, deep caves, which contain a variety of tunnels, narrow streams, lakes, and waterfalls.

LOCATION Lower Alps of the Provence Alpes region, southeast France

TYPE Karst

RIVERS Drôme and Isère

avango Delta

Okavango River starts in Angola ends in a huge inland delta called the vango Delta. The river water pours into the a, creating plant-rich wetlands that remain mpy throughout the year.

ATION Ngamiland District of northern swana, to the northern Kalahari Desert

E Delta and swamp

ER Okavango

Lakes

Lakes are bodies of water that are created when surface water collects in a depression. Some are as shallow as a pond, while others are about half a mile (1 km) deep. Lakes may contain salt water or fresh water. Some have outlets to carry water away, while others do not.

Great Slave Lake

The Great Slave Lake has a rocky shore with wide bays and many islands. Most of the land is covered with dense coniferous forests. This lake remains frozen for eight months of the year.

LOCATION Northwest Canada, east of the Mackenzie Mountains
AREA 11,029 sq miles (28,565 sq km)
MAXIMUM DEPTH 2,015 ft (615 m)
OUTLET Mackenzie River

Great Bear Lake

The largest lake solely within Canadian territory, Great Bear Lake extends into the Arctic Circle in the north. The evergreen forests along its southern shores are home to grizzly bears.

LOCATION Northwest Canada, on the Arctic Circle
AREA 12,025 sq miles (31,150 sq km)
MAXIMUM DEPTH 1,465 ft (445 m)
OUTLET Great Bear River

eat Salt Lake

This is the largest inland saltwater body in the western hemisphere. This lake has no outlet, so it can lose water only by evaporation, which leads to the buildup of minerals, making the lake extremely salty. It is surrounded by great areas of sand, salt flats, and salt marshes.

Boulders coated with salt crystals

LOCATION Western Rocky Mountains, northern Utah

AREA 2,000 sq miles (5,000 sq km)

MAXIMUM DEPTH 39 ft (12 m)

OUTLET None

e Ladoga

ope's largest lake, Ladoga lies in a hollow gouged out by glaciers. The water is est near the high, rocky cliffs of the hern shores, while in the south, the lake uch shallower and has a low shoreline. entire lake freezes between the months anuary and May.

LOCATION Karelia region of northwestern Russia, to the east of the Baltic Sea

AREA 6,825 sq miles (17,675 sq km)

MAXIMUM DEPTH 755 ft (230 m)

OUTLET Neva River

Lake Baikal

The oldest lake in the world, Baikal formed about 25 million years ago. It continues to widen at a rate of about 1 in (2½ cm) every year. It is also the Earth's deepest lake, containing 20 percent of the planet's entire surface fresh water.

LOCATION Russia, south of the Central Siberian Plateau, near Mongolia

AREA 12,160 sq miles (31,500 sq km)

MAXIMUM DEPTH 5,715 ft (1,740 m)

OUTLET Angara River

Caspian Sea

The Caspian Sea is the Earth's largest inland b of water. It was once open sea, but got landloc following the movement of tectonic plates. Its water level is constantly rising and falling due climate change, which affects the level of the r flowing into it and the rate of evaporation.

Dead Sea

ATION On the borders of
baijan, Iran, Kazakhstan, Russia,
Turkmenistan

A	143,000 sq miles (371,000 sq km)
KIMUM DEPTH	3,120 ft (950 m)
LET	None

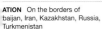

Lake Vostok

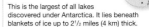

This is the largest of all lakes
discovered under Antarctica. It lies beneath
blankets of ice up to 2¹/₂ miles (4 km) thick.

LOCATION	Under the eastern Antarctic Ice Sheet
AREA	5,791 sq miles (15,000 sq km)
MAXIMUM DEPTH	3,000 ft (900 m)
OUTLET	None

is the world's lowest lake and, at
0 ft (400 m) below sea level, the lowest
t on the Earth's surface. Because of the
emely high rate of evaporation, the Dead
is shrinking rapidly, its level lowering by
ut 3½ ft (1 m) every year. This evaporation
gives the lake a very high salt content—
too salty, in fact, for anything to live in it,
ch is how it got its name.

ATION North of the Red Sea,
ered by Israel and Jordan

A	310 sq miles (810 sq km)
KIMUM DEPTH	1,085 ft (330 m)
LET	None

Wetlands

When water collects on land and cannot drain, it builds up and forms flooded areas called wetlands. Lagoons are areas of shallow sea separated by islands or reefs, while swamps are wooded areas submerged in water. Marshes are similar to swamps, but they are covered with grasses and reeds.

Great Dismal Swamp

The bottom of this swamp is covered with fallen trees and other plants. At its center is a circular freshwater lake called Lake Drummond. These wetlands are unusual in being located above sea level, whereas most swamps are found in low-lying natural basins or craters.

LOCATION About 25 miles (40 km) inland from the Atlantic Ocean, in North Carolina and Virginia

TYPE Swamp

AREA 600 sq miles (1,550 sq km)

erglades

er flowing from Lake Okeechobee
os slowly through the low-lying land
ard the Gulf of Mexico. This creates
etland with wide areas of sawgrass.
 edges of this grass are so sharp they
 cut through cloth.

:ATION From Lake Okeechobee
lorida Bay, Florida

E Swamp and marsh

A 4,000 sq miles (10,000 sq km)

nos wetlands

ry May, heavy rains flood the Llanos
ands, creating islands of forests. These
erlogged areas are important habitats
vater birds, supporting about 90 percent
e world's population of the endangered
let ibis.

LOCATION Orinoco River and its
tributaries in western Venezuela

TYPE Swamp and marsh

AREA 4,000 sq miles (10,000 sq km)

Pantanal

The world's largest freshwater wetland, the Pantanal occupies about a third of the upper basin of the Paraguay River. When the river floods every year, this swamp acts as a sponge and soaks up the excess water.

LOCATION Mato Grosso and Mato Grosso do Sul states of Brazil, extending into Bolivia and Paraguay

TYPE Swamp and marsh

AREA 50,000 sq miles (130,000 sq km)

Camargue

This wetland is famous for its unique breed of white horses and for its birds, including greater flamingos and black-winged stilts.

LOCATION Rhône Delta, France

TYPE Lagoon and marsh

AREA 330 sq miles (850 sq km)

Sudd

These marshes are a landscape of reed-beds and papyrus, with areas of water that are choked by dense mats of floating wa hyacinth. An incomplete and abandoned cana project on its eastern side has left a huge trou which blocks the migration of large mammals

LOCATION White Nile River, southern Sudan

TYPE Marsh

AREA 13,300 sq miles (34,500 sq km)

...ndarbans

...is network of estuaries (wetlands where a
...er meets a sea) and tidal rivers surrounds flat,
...arshy islands covered with thick forests. The
...gion supports a variety of wildlife, including
...otted deer and the Bengal tiger.

LOCATION Between Kolkata, India,
and Chittagong, Bangladesh

TYPE Swamp and marsh

AREA 685 sq miles (1,770 sq km)

...oorong

...e Coorong is a long, shallow lagoon that
...separated from the Southern Ocean by a
...rrow sand dune peninsula. It is one of the
...st sites for bird-watching in Australia, as
...s home to more than 230 species of bird.

LOCATION Mouth of the Murray
River, Australia

TYPE Lagoon

AREA 80 sq miles (200 sq km)

Glaciers

Glaciers are giant masses of ice formed by the piling up of snow over time. Most glaciers, except for massive icecaps and ice sheets, move down a mountain area and flow into a valley. When a glacier reaches the sea, chunks break off, forming icebergs.

Hubbard Glacier

The Hubbard Glacier has been advancing for over a century. It threatens to block off a narrow strip of water near the Alaskan coast called Russell Fjord. If this fjord gets permanently blocked, it could overflow and flood the surrounding land.

Malaspina Glacier

The Malaspina Glacier features the largest piedmont lobe in the world. This glacial type occurs when a valley glacier—formed when a glacier moves down a mountain into a valley—spreads out onto a low, flat area.

LOCATION	Coast of St. Elias Mountains, Alaska
TYPE	Piedmont lobe
AREA	1,500 sq miles (3,900 sq km)

Greenland Ice Sheet

Covering 80 percent of Greenland, this ice sheet is the largest ice mass in the northern hemisphere. Most northern Atlantic icebergs originate from this glacier, which contains 10 percent of the world's fresh water. It has an average thickness of 5,900 ft (1,790 m).

CATION St. Elias Mountains,
nada, through southeastern Alaska

PE Valley glacier

EA 1,350 sq miles (3,500 sq km)

Vatnajökull Icecap

The largest glacier in Europe,
Vatnajökull completely covers the
mountainous Icelandic terrain it sits on.
It lies on top of several volcanoes. The heat
from these causes the icecap's base to melt,
creating lakes beneath it.

LOCATION Southeast Iceland

TYPE Icecap

AREA 3,100 sq miles (8,100 sq km)

ATION Greenland in the
c Circle

E Ice sheet

A 668,000 sq miles (1.73 million sq km)

Antarctic Ice Sheet

The largest mass of ice on the Earth,
the Antarctic Ice Sheet weighs so much that
it pushes the Earth's crust down by about
2,955 ft (900 m). This glacier holds more
than 70 percent of the world's fresh water.

LOCATION Antarctica

TYPE Ice sheet

AREA 5.3 million sq miles (13.7 million sq km)

Antarctic winters are

so harsh

that only a few birds, including emperor penguins, can breed during this time

THE COOL COLONY
To survive on the cold Antarctic Ice Sheet, emperor penguins form breeding colonies in areas that are sheltered from the wind by ice cliffs and icebergs. They also huddle together in groups, taking turns to move to the center so that each penguin stays warm.

Glacial features

As glaciers move through and wear away mountainous regions, they create unique landforms. Great masses of ice can carve out valleys, flatten mountains, and pick up rocks and carry them for great distances. Some glacial features only become apparent when glaciers melt and disappear.

Yorkshire boulder

Glaciers can carry huge boulders over large distances. The Yorkshire boulder was carried by a glacier and then dropped on top of younger rock when the glacier melted. Such rocks are known as erratics.

LOCATION	Yorkshire, UK
TYPE	Erratic
GLACIER	Ice sheet

Muldalen hanging valley

Large glaciers are often fed by smaller flows of ice called tributary glaciers. While the large glacier gouges out a deep valley, the tributary carves a much smaller, higher "hanging valley" above the main valley. As with many hanging valleys, a waterfall sometimes flows from Muldalen down into the main valley.

LOCATION	Muldalen, near Tafiord, Norway
TYPE	Hanging valley
GLACIER	Hanging valley glacier

ew Bay

...umlins are long, oval mounds of sediment ...t have been smoothed in the direction of a ...cier's flow. In Clew Bay, clusters of drumlins ...pear as islands in the sea.

LOCATION	County Mayo, Ireland
TYPE	Drumlin
GLACIER	Valley glacier

...yllefjord cirque

...rque is a curved, bowl-shaped feature at the ...d of a developing valley glacier. It is formed by ...sion. The cirque at Gryllefjord has an arête— ...ng, thin ridge separating two cirques.

...CATION	Gryllefjord, Norway
...PE	Cirque
...CIER	Cirque glacier

Dolma La Pass lake

This lake in Dolma La Pass was formed when an ice block broke off from a glacier and got buried in the ground. It then melted, and created a kettle hole that filled with water to form a kettle lake.

LOCATION	Dolma La Pass, Tibet
TYPE	Kettle lake
GLACIER	Valley glacier

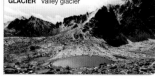

Deserts

Areas of land that receive an average rainfall of less than 10 in (250 mm) a year are called deserts. Hot deserts have high temperatures year-round, while in cold deserts, the winters are freezing.

FOCUS ON...
LAND FORM
Deserts feature a variety of landscape from mountains and plateaus to plains.

Great Basin Desert

Its high altitude and northerly position make the Great Basin Desert the only cold desert in the US. Its vegetation includes sagebrush, blackbrush, and shadscale, along with a few cacti.

LOCATION Oregon, Idaho, Nevada, Utah, Wyoming, Colorado, and California

TYPE Sandy and gravelly

AREA 158,000 sq miles (409,000 sq km)

RAINFALL 10 in (250 mm)

Atacama Desert

This is the driest place on the Earth, and includes stretches of land where rain has never been recorded. In certain areas of this desert, coastal fogs form, providing some moisture for the growth of plants such as cacti.

LOCATION The coast of northern Chile, west of the Andes, between Arica and Vallena

TYPE Rocky and salty

AREA 40,600 sq miles (105,200 sq km)

RAINFALL Less than $^3/_5$ in (15 mm)

...some deserts, wind covers ...rocks in a dark coating called ...rt varnish. Many of these ...ks feature ancient rock art.

▲ Inselbergs, also known as monadnocks, are isolated hills that stand out above the flat desert surface around them.

▲ Desert sand dunes are hills of sand made by wind blowing over the desert. They occur in varying shapes and sizes.

...hara Desert

...Sahara is the Earth's largest hot desert, ...ering an area about the size of the US. ...s reddish sand and is famous for its ergs, ...nd seas. These areas of sand can be up ...28 ft (100 m) deep, and feature different ...pes of dunes.

...ATION From the Atlantic Ocean to ...Red Sea, covering most of northern Africa

...E Sandy, gravelly, and stony

...A 3.5 million sq miles (9 million sq km)

...NFALL ⁴/₅–16 in (20–400 mm)

Namib Desert

The Namib Desert is situated on the coast, where moisture from sea fogs supports the growth of some unique plants. These include the *Welwitschia mirabilis*, which is famous for producing only two leaves in its lifetime that can span hundreds of years.

LOCATION	Atlantic coast of Namibia, extending into southern Angola in the north
TYPE	Gravelly and sandy
AREA	12,000 sq miles (31,000 sq km)
RAINFALL	³/₅–4 in (15–100 mm)

Kalahari Desert

Sandwiched between the Orange River in the south and the Zambezi in the north, this desert is dominated by sandy ridges, along with dry lake beds and wide areas of salt-covered ground. The Kalahari is home to the nomadic San people, whose population is about 40,000.

LOCATION Southern Botswana, extending west into Namibia and south into South Africa

TYPE Sandy

AREA 350,000 sq miles (900,000 sq km)

RAINFALL 5–20 in (125–500 mm)

Arabian Peninsula

The Arabian Peninsula contains some of the largest sandy desert areas in the world. This includes the Ar Rub 'al Khali, or Empty Quarter, in the south, which covers an area about the size of France.

LOCATION From Syria to Yemen and Oman, east of the Red Sea

TYPE Sandy and gravelly

AREA 900,000 sq miles (2.3 million sq km)

RAINFALL 2–8 in (50–200 mm)

i Desert

Featuring a varied landscape, from rocky mountains to wide valleys and plains, the Gobi actually has very little sand. The central region of the desert is stony, with very little plant life, and the western region is extremely dry.

LOCATION Across southern Mongolia and the north of China as far as the Great Wall

TYPE Stony, gravelly, and sandy

AREA 500,000 sq miles (1.3 million sq km)

RAINFALL $^{1}/_{2}$–10 in (10–250 mm)

at Sandy Desert

most Australian deserts, the sand here ight red because it is coated in iron oxides, h is similar to rust. The Great Sandy Desert own for its dunes, which the wind constantly ges into new shapes.

LOCATION North of western Australia, extending as far as the Indian Ocean

TYPE Gravelly and sandy

AREA 130,000 sq miles (340,000 sq km)

RAINFALL 10–12 in (250–300 mm)

LANDFORMS OF MOJAVE
Found within the Mojave Desert of California, Death Valley is the lowest, hottest, and driest part of the North American continent. Large rocks, called "sailing stones," appear to move across the ground of this desert—no one knows how.

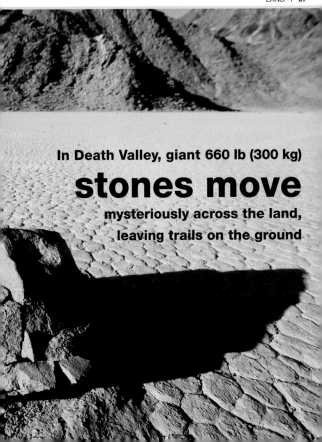

In Death Valley, giant 660 lb (300 kg)

stones move

mysteriously across the land,
leaving trails on the ground

Forests

A forest is an area with a high density of tre
Covering about 30 percent of the Earth's
surface, forests are found in regions with
enough heat and rainfall to support tree
growth. The trees provide oxygen and foo
rich habitats for a wide variety of animal

FOCUS ON...
TREES

Forests are made up of two main types of tree—evergreen and deciduous.

▲ Evergreen trees, such as pine trees, never shed all their leaves. They remain green throughout the year.

▲ Maple, birch, and other deciduous trees shed their leaves in the fall and remain bare all winter. The leaves grow back in the spring.

North American boreal forest

Boreal forests are found in the colder parts of the northern hemisphere. The North American boreal forest is covered in snow for most of the year. Its tree canopy consists mainly of black and white spruce, as these trees can survive this extreme cold. It is bordered to the north by the Arctic tundra where conditions are too harsh to support tree growth.

LOCATION	Central Alaska to central Labrador, Canada
TYPE	Boreal forest
AREA	2.4 million sq miles (6.25 million sq km)

ifornia coniferous forest

se forests are famous for being home
ne world's largest tree species—the giant
uoia. These trees may grow for over 2,000
s and reach almost 328 ft (100 m) in height.

ATION Sierra Nevada, California

PE Evergreen temperate forest

EA 16,800 sq miles
600 sq km)

Pacific northwest forest

High rainfall and coastal fogs create
ideal conditions for the growth of some
huge trees in this forest, such as the redwood,
Douglas fir, sitka spruce, and western hemlock.

LOCATION The Gulf of Alaska to northern
California and Canada

TYPE Temperate rainforest

AREA 463,000 sq miles (1.2 million sq km)

azon rainforest

largest area of tropical rainforest in the
ld, the Amazon rainforest covers much
he basin of the Amazon River. More than
of the world's species of plant, animal,
insect live in this rainforest.

LOCATION From the Andes,
South America, to the Atlantic Ocean

TYPE Tropical rainforest

AREA 2.3 million sq miles (6 million sq km)

Some tribes living
deep inside the
Amazon rainforest
have never had
contact with the
outside world.

European mixed forest

This type of forest occurs in much of
the lowland and hill country in Europe,
particularly in Central Europe. Depending on the
weather pattern, type of soil, and drainage of
rainwater, a variety of trees grow here, including
oak, beech, lime, ash, elm, birch, and alder.

LOCATION From the British Isles
to western Russia

TYPE Deciduous temperate and evergreen
temperate forests

AREA 1.6 million sq miles (4 million sq km)

Eurasian boreal forest

Central African rainforest

The rainforests of central Africa
make up more than 80 percent of the
continent's total area of rainforest.
About 11,000 plant species, and
more than 400 species of mammal,
are found in the rainforests of the
Democratic Republic of Congo.
The mountain forests of Uganda,
Rwanda, and Burundi are home
to the famous mountain gorilla.

LOCATION Cameroon, Equatorial Guinea;
and Gabon to Uganda and Burundi

TYPE Tropical rainforest

AREA 733,000 sq miles (1.9 million sq km)

Although this forest consists mostly of evergreen conifers, such as the Norway spruce and the Scots pine, some parts of the forest support deciduous trees such as larch, birch, alder, and rowan. Some areas even feature a mix of both types of tree growing together.

LOCATION Western Scandinavia, across northern Europe and Asia, to the Pacific Ocean

TYPE Boreal forest

AREA 3.4 million sq miles (8.75 million sq km)

Madagascan rainforest

Most of this rainforest lies on the eastern side of the island of Madagascar, which broke off from mainland Africa about 135 million years ago. Because of the island's isolation, about 80 percent of its plants and 95 percent of its 300 reptile species—including two-thirds of the world's chameleons—are not found anywhere else.

LOCATION Masoala Peninsula, Madagascar

TYPE Tropical rainforest

AREA 14,670 sq miles (38,000 sq km)

Northeast Asian mixed forest

This mixed forest mostly features cedar pine, black fir, and local species of spruce, ash, maple, linden, and walnut. Its wildlife includes mammals such as the musk deer and the rare Siberian tiger.

LOCATION Northeast China, through Korea, southeast Russia, and northern Japan

TYPE Deciduous temperate and evergreen temperate forests

AREA 1.2 million sq miles (3.2 million sq km)

rtheast Australian rainforest

s forest grows on the eastern slopes
he country's coastal mountain ranges,
ere the average annual rainfall is more
n 59 in (150 cm). Its trees range from
ft (20 m) to 130 ft (40 m) tall.

LOCATION	Northeast Queensland, from Cape York south to the Connors Range
TYPE	Tropical rainforest
AREA	4,000 sq miles (10,500 sq km)

llemi pine forest

e Wollemi pine is a survivor
n a 200 million-year-old group
lants. It was thought to be
nct—with the youngest fossils
ng back two million years—until
4, when a living plant was
covered in an isolated part of
stralia. Fewer than 100 adult
s are known to exist in the wild.

CATION Western edge of
Sydney Basin, Australia

PE Temperate rainforest

EA Limited and secret location
hin the Wollemi National Park

Grasslands

Grasslands are areas where there is not enough rain for many tree to grow, but there is enough to prevent deserts from forming. Ther are two types—temperate grasslands, which have hot summers, cold winters, and year-round rainfall; and tropical grasslands, or savanna, which have wet and dry seasons.

Great Plains

The Great Plains is by far the largest area of grassland in North America. Its land is so fertile that most of it is now used for agriculture. Only one percent is still in its natural, wild state.

LOCATION North America, between the Rocky Mountains and Mississippi River

TYPE Temperate

AREA 1.2 million sq miles (3 million sq km)

Pampas

This huge plain has varying landscapes. The eastern side has a mild climate all year round, and features pampas grass, which is known for its tall stems with silky, featherlike flowers. Toward the Andes, the land is extreme dry and turns into a semi-desert.

LOCATION Northern Argentina and Uruguay, from the Andes foothills to the Atlantic Ocean

TYPE Temperate

AREA 270,000 sq miles (700,000 sq km)

Serengeti Plains

These plains feature a mix of grasslands and forests, and have the largest populations of grazing animals in Africa. Every summer, when the grasses dry up, more than 1.3 million blue wildebeest, 200,000 zebras, and 40,000 Thomson's gazelles migrate across the Serengeti in search of fresh grass and drinking water.

LOCATION From northwest Tanzania, east of Lake Victoria, to southwest Kenya

TYPE Tropical

AREA 8,900 sq miles (23,000 sq km)

Central Asian steppes

Extreme changes in temperature are common in this region, but animals here are adapted to cope. For example, saiga antelope develop a thick, woolly coat to keep warm in the winter and a thin, reddish coat during the summer.

LOCATION From Ukraine, through Russia and Kazakhstan to Mongolia and China

TYPE Temperate

AREA 965,000 sq miles (2.5 million sq km)

Australian savanna

Made up of dense, scattered trees, the savanna forms a band between the hot desert interior of Australia and the forests on its north coast. The region has cool, dry winters, and hot, humid summers.

LOCATION North of western Australia, through Northern Territory, into Queensland

TYPE Tropical

AREA 463,500 sq miles (1.2 million sq km)

Tundra

The term tundra is used to describe a vast and almost treeless landscape that covers about 20 percent of the Earth's land surfa The ground remains frozen for most of the year. In some areas, t top layer thaws during the spring and the summer. Where the grour remains frozen for at least two years, it is known as permafrost.

North American tundra

Although it is mostly flat and barren, the North American tundra does feature some landforms such as polygons (geometrical patterns on the soil), pingos (ice mounds), and even a few mountain ranges. In the spring, the ice and snow melt to show lichens, mosses, and Arctic flowers.

LOCATION From Alaska through northern Canada; Greenland's coastal regions

AREA 2 million sq miles (5.3 million sq km)

TEMPERATURE -76°F–75°F (-60°C–24°C)

RAINFALL 2–8 in (50–200 mm)

rasian tundra

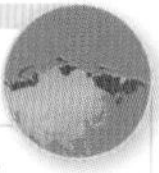

s region features a variety of landscapes,
n the freezing damp plains of Siberia to
island groups of the southern Arctic Ocean.
umber of small, long-lived plants, such as
sses and rushes, are found here. These
ts grow only during a short, 90-day period
n May to July. Many migratory animals arrive
ng these warmer months.

LOCATION From Iceland in the west,
through northern Scandinavia, Russia,
and Siberia

AREA 1.3 million sq miles (3.3 million sq km)

TEMPERATURE -76°F–77°F (-60°C–25°C)

RAINFALL 8–12 in (200–300 mm)

During the summer,
more than 200 million
breeding birds, including
ducks and geese,
migrate to the
Eurasian tundra.

TUNDRA COLORS
In the tundra, the temperature rises during the summer, and the frozen topsoil melts to form small pools. The ground thaws just enough to allow plants to reproduce, before the winter sets in. When the spring arrives, these plants flower, and the region shows splashes of color.

In the summer, **the Sun never sets** over the tundra

Agricultural areas

Farming began in the Middle East around 10,000 years ago, and today, it actively involves two billion people worldwide. Farming ca be arable (growing crops) or pastoral (rearing livestock such as ca and pigs). Farming practices depend on many things, including climate, altitude, soil condition, economics, and local traditions.

Cereal cultivation

The first plants to be domesticated were cereals—grasses that are grown for their edible seeds or grains. Cereals are an important source of energy and are grown in large quantities. Wheat, rice, and corn together account for over half the world's food. Other popular cereals are rye, oats, and barley.

TYPE	Arable
AREA	14 million sq miles (36 million sq km)
MAIN COUNTRIES	China, US, India, and Russia

Cattle farming

Cattle are an important source of meat, but a also kept for their milk. The largest cattle farm are found where there are vast areas of open land, such as North America, South America, and Australia.

TYPE	Pastoral
AREA	11.2 million sq miles (29 million sq km
MAIN COUNTRIES	US, China, Brazil, Argentina, and Australia

ce cultivation

wing rice requires lots of water. In
areas, rice is grown in terraces—levels cut
the hillsides to keep soil and water in place.
e was first cultivated in Asia, which remains
world's largest producer of this crop.

PE Arable

EA 4.6 million sq miles (12 million sq km)

N COUNTRIES China, India, Indonesia,
gladesh, and Vietnam

Plantation agriculture

A plantation is a large estate where only
one type of crop is grown. Most large-
scale commercial crops that are grown in
warm climates are produced in plantations.
These include tea, coffee, bananas, palm oil,
cocoa, sugar cane, and cotton.

TYPE Arable

AREA 3.1 million sq miles (8 million sq km)

MAIN COUNTRIES Malaysia,
Brazil, Mexico, India, and Cuba

xed farming

his type of farming, farmers grow and
a range of crops and livestock, rather
concentrating on a single product. This
uces farmer's risk of losses, for example, if a
ticular crop gets infected or if animals get sick.

TYPE Arable and pastoral

AREA 21 million sq miles (54 million sq km)

MAIN COUNTRIES China, India, US,
Russia, and France

Urban areas

Today, half the world's population live in urban areas—cities and towns—rather than in the countryside. About three percent of the Earth's land surface is urban, and this figure is likely to double over the next 20 years. Cities are centers of culture, transportation, trade, and technology.

São Paulo

One of the world's fastest-growing cities, São Paulo is located near large deposits of iron ore, which led to its industrial development. Its links to Santos, the busiest port in Latin America make it a major center of transportation.

COUNTRY	Brazil
AREA	585 sq miles (1,525 sq km)
POPULATION	11.3 million

New York City

The largest city in the US, New York is one of the world's leading cultural and financial centers. It is also famous for its skyline, which is made up of many extremely tall buildings called skyscrapers, such as the Empire State Building.

COUNTRY	US
AREA	470 sq miles (1,215 sq km)
POPULATION	8.2 million

...don

...city of London was established
...ne Romans more than 2,000 years ago. It is
...ted on the Thames River, which is famous for
...many bridges built over it, including Tower
...ge. The capital city of the UK, London is
...bal center of finance and theater.

...NTRY UK

...A 605 sq miles (1,570 sq km)

...ULATION 12.8 million

New Delhi

As India's capital city, New Delhi is a key
political, financial, and industrial center.
The Rashtrapati Bhavan—the official residence
of the president of India—is located here, as
are other important government buildings.

COUNTRY India

AREA 575 sq miles (1,485 sq km)

POPULATION 12.3 million

...yo

...city of Tokyo is part of a huge urban area
...more than 30 million inhabitants. It is often
...cted by earthquakes because it is located
...re four tectonic plates meet.

COUNTRY Japan

AREA 845 sq miles (2,190 sq km)

POPULATION 13.2 million

Ocean

Oceans cover about two-thirds of the Earth's surface, at an average depth of 12,100 ft (3,700 m). The Earth's oceans formed more than three billion years ago. Until the first life-forms emerged onto land 450 million years ago, life was found only in the oceans. Over time, the oceans have grown and shrunk as the Earth's internal forces have moved the continents around. The movement of heat and moisture between the oceans and the atmosphere plays a crucial role in shaping the world's climates.

A GLOW IN THE DARK
Many sea animals, such as this comb jelly, produce light in the dark depths of the ocean. This light helps them to find and attract prey, or to signal to other animals.

Ocean currents

Ocean water is constantly moving, both at the surface and far below the waves, circulating warm water from the equator and cold water from the poles. The patterns of this movement are called ocean currents. These currents are influenced by several factors, including the Earth's rotation, the winds, and tidal changes in sea level.

Currents and gyres

The combination of wind blowing over the oceans and the rotation of the Earth makes surface water swirl clockwise in the northern hemisphere and counterclockwise in the southern hemisphere. These swirling patterns, called gyres, carry warm tropical water away from the equator and colder water toward it.

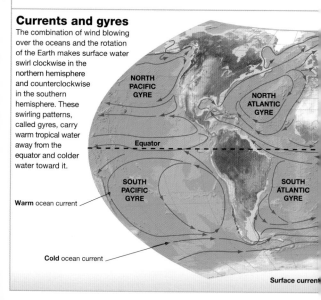

NORTH PACIFIC GYRE

NORTH ATLANTIC GYRE

Equator

SOUTH PACIFIC GYRE

SOUTH ATLANTIC GYRE

Warm ocean current

Cold ocean current

Surface current

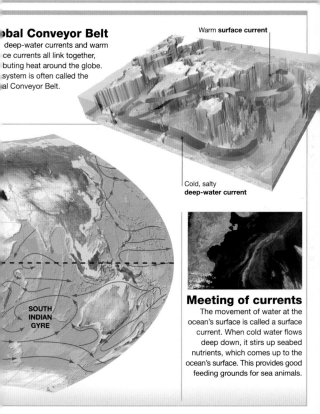

bal Conveyor Belt

deep-water currents and warm
ce currents all link together,
buting heat around the globe.
system is often called the
al Conveyor Belt.

Warm **surface current**

Cold, salty
deep-water current

SOUTH
INDIAN
GYRE

Meeting of currents

The movement of water at the
ocean's surface is called a surface
current. When cold water flows
deep down, it stirs up seabed
nutrients, which comes up to the
ocean's surface. This provides good
feeding grounds for sea animals.

Seas and oceans

The Earth has five oceans. Around their edges are smaller bodies of water, including seas, bays, and gulfs. Together, oceans and seas cover more than two-thirds of the Earth's surface. Below the waves, the ocean floors are made up of various features, such as mountain ranges, deep plains and trenches, and coral reefs.

Arctic Ocean

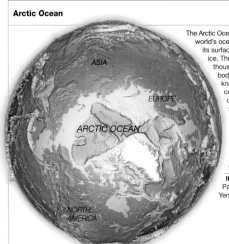

The Arctic Ocean is the smallest of the world's oceans. About one-third of its surface is permanently covered in ice. The Arctic Ocean also contains thousands of icebergs and larger bodies called ice islands. Ships known as icebreakers, which can cut through the ice, create channels for commercial ships to pass through this ice-covered ocean.

AREA 5.4 million sq miles (14 million sq km)
MAXIMUM DEPTH 15,305 ft (4,665 m)
INFLOWS Atlantic and Pacific oceans; Mackenzie, Ob, Yenisey, Lena, and Kolyma rivers

ukchi Sea

ter low in salt content flows from the Pacific
ean into the colder, more saline (salty) water
he Chukchi Sea. Rich in nutrients, this mixed
ter supports a wide variety of marine life,
ch includes large populations of walrus
I several species of seals.

AREA 225,000 sq miles
(582,000 sq km)

MAXIMUM DEPTH 360 ft (110 m)

INFLOWS Bering and East Siberian seas,
and Arctic Basin

rents Sea

ike other Arctic seas, the Barents Sea
nains mostly ice-free through the year.
floor is rich in invertebrates, such as
cucumbers, feather stars, and starfish.

EA 542,000 sq miles (1.4 million sq km)

XIMUM DEPTH 2,000 ft (600 m)

LOWS Norwegian Sea and Arctic Basin

White Sea

The White Sea is an almost landlocked
part of the Arctic Ocean. Its floor is
broken up by troughs and ridges.

AREA 35,000 sq miles (90,000 sq km)

MAXIMUM DEPTH 1,115 ft (340 m)

INFLOWS Barents Sea; Onega and Northern
Dvina rivers

Atlantic Ocean

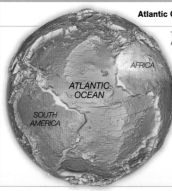

The world's second largest ocean, the Atlantic has several tributary seas. A massive mountain range, called the Mid-Atlantic Ridg[e] covers almost one-third of the ocean floor. T[he] range has basins on either side, some of which contain large volcanoes.

AREA 29.7 million sq miles (77 million sq k[m])
MAXIMUM DEPTH 28,230 ft (8,605 m)
INFLOWS Arctic and Southern oceans; Mediterranean Sea; St. Lawrence, Mississippi, Orinoco, Amazon, Paraná, Congo, Niger, Loire, and Rhine rivers

Black Sea

An almost landlocked body of water, the Black Sea mostly occupies a deep, broad basin separating Europe from Asia.

AREA 163,000 sq miles (422,000 sq km)
MAXIMUM DEPTH 7,200 ft (2,200 m)
INFLOWS Sea of Azov, Mediterranean Sea; Danube, Dniester, Dnieper, and Kizil Irmak rivers

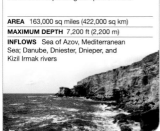

Mediterranean Sea

The world's largest inland sea, the Mediterrane[an] was separated from the Atlantic Ocean to the west when the Earth's sea level dropped, abou[t] million years ago. Over the next two million ye[ars] the region flooded, the water levels rose, and [the] sea linked to the Atlantic again.

ltic Sea

out 8,000 years ago, the ice sheet covered Scandinavia melted, submerging region under water. The Baltic Sea is what ains of that water. Nine countries have their stline on this sea.

SEA	149,000 sq miles (386,000 sq km)
MAXIMUM DEPTH	1,475 ft (450 m)
LOWS	Vistula, Oder, and stern Dvina rivers

EA	965,000 sq miles (million sq km)
KIMUM DEPTH	16,075 ft (4,900 m)
LOWS	Atlantic Ocean; Black Sea; , Rhône, Po, and Ebro rivers

Hudson Bay

This large, shallow body of water has a rocky eastern coast with high cliffs, but its other shores are marshy and low. High amounts of nutrients are dissolved in its waters. These support a variety of creatures, including beluga whales, which enter the bay during the summer season.

AREA	316,000 sq miles (819,000 sq km)
MAXIMUM DEPTH	886 ft (270 m)
INFLOWS	Albany, Churchill, Moose, Nelson, Severn, and Grande Rivière de la Baleine rivers

Sargasso Sea

This is the only sea of the northern Atlantic that is not bordered by land. It is created by three currents around its edge—the Canaries Current, the North Equatorial Current, and the Gulf Stream. The Sargasso Sea is named for the wide mats of sargassum, a yellow-brown seaweed, that float on its surface. This seaweed supports a variety of animal life.

AREA	2 million sq miles (5.2 million sq km)
MAXIMUM DEPTH	23,000 ft (7,000 m)
INFLOWS	None

The sargassum seaweed has tiny gas-filled bladders, allowing it to float on the water surface

Gulf of Mexico

This oval basin contains mostly shallow waters. Mangrove swamps, tidal marshes, beaches, lagoons, and estuaries are found along its coasts. The Mississippi River carries a huge volume of sand and silt into the Gulf of Mexico. These sediments are deposited on the seafloor, forming an enormous fan-shaped delta with wide salt marshes.

AREA	615,000 sq miles (1.6 million sq km)
MAXIMUM DEPTH	17,060 ft (5,200 m)
INFLOWS	Caribbean Sea; Mississippi, Brazos, Colorado, Alabama, Apalachicola, and Rio Grande rivers

Caribbean Sea

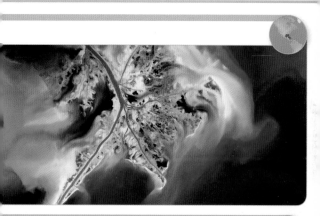

The sea, its numerous islands—many of which are volcanic—and neighboring coastlines make up the Caribbean region. Most of the islands, as well as some of the mainland coasts, are lined with coral reefs that support a rich variety of fish and invertebrates, including spiny lobsters and conches.

AREA 1.1 million sq miles (2.75 million sq km)

MAXIMUM DEPTH 25,215 ft (7,685 m)

INFLOWS Atlantic Ocean; Magdalena, Coco, Patuca, and Motagua rivers

Indian Ocean

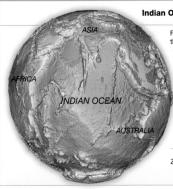

Formed over the last 120 million years, the Indian Ocean is one of the world's youngest ocean basins. Its mostly warm waters create ideal conditions for a large variety of marine life. Twice every year, the monsoon winds reverse the flow of its currents, bringing up nutrient-rich water from the ocean's depths. This pattern is unique to the Indian Ocean.

AREA 26.5 million sq miles (69 million sq km)

MAXIMUM DEPTH 23,815 ft (7,260 m)

INFLOWS Ganges, Indus, Tigris, Euphrates, Zambezi, Limpopo, and Murray rivers

Arabian Sea

The Arabian Sea occupies the northwestern part of the Indian Ocean. In addition to supporting a huge fishing industry, it is also an important trade route linking the Red Sea with the Persian Gulf.

AREA 1.5 million sq miles (3.9 million sq km)

MAXIMUM DEPTH 19,030 ft (5,800 m)

INFLOWS Indus and Narmada rivers

...daman Sea

...heast of the Bay of Bengal, the
...aman Sea is separated from the bay
...e Andaman and Nicobar islands. This
...n is close to three tectonic plates—
...ndia plate, the Burma plate, and the
...da Megathrust—and is often affected
...arthquakes.

...A 308,000 sq miles (798,000 sq km)

...IMUM DEPTH 12,390 ft (3,775 m)

...OWS Bay of Bengal, Strait of Malacca;
...addy and Salween rivers

...sian Gulf

...warm, salty sea is known for the huge
...serves found beneath its floor. Its eastern
...e is mountainous, while its western shore
...many islands, lagoons, and tidal flats. Many
...cial islands have been built along its coast,
... as the Palm Islands in the UAE, which
...shaped like palm trees.

AREA 93,000 sq miles
(241,000 sq km)

MAXIMUM DEPTH 360 ft (110 m)

INFLOWS Tigris, Euphrates, and Karun rivers

Pacific Ocean

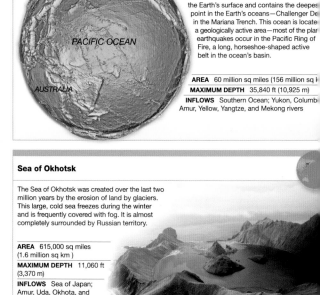

PACIFIC OCEAN

AUSTRALIA

The largest ocean in the world, the Pacific covers more than one-third of the Earth's surface and contains the deepest point in the Earth's oceans—Challenger De in the Mariana Trench. This ocean is locate a geologically active area—most of the plan earthquakes occur in the Pacific Ring of Fire, a long, horseshoe-shaped active belt in the ocean's basin.

AREA 60 million sq miles (156 million sq k

MAXIMUM DEPTH 35,840 ft (10,925 m)

INFLOWS Southern Ocean; Yukon, Columb Amur, Yellow, Yangtze, and Mekong rivers

Sea of Okhotsk

The Sea of Okhotsk was created over the last two million years by the erosion of land by glaciers. This large, cold sea freezes during the winter and is frequently covered with fog. It is almost completely surrounded by Russian territory.

AREA 615,000 sq miles (1.6 million sq km)

MAXIMUM DEPTH 11,060 ft (3,370 m)

INFLOWS Sea of Japan; Amur, Uda, Okhota, and Penzhina rivers

uth China Sea

South China Sea stretches for more
1,680 miles (2,700 km) around Asia's
nland. The Gulf of Thailand, which branches
from the sea, has 42 forest-covered islands,
ch rise from the sea as rock formations.
se islands make up a marine park called
Ang Thong National Park.

AREA 1.4 million sq miles
(3.7 million sq km)

MAXIMUM DEPTH 16,455 ft (5,015 m)

INFLOWS Xi Jiang, Mekong, Red, Tha Chin,
and Chao Phraya rivers

ral Sea

nous for the world's largest coral reef—the
at Barrier Reef—the Coral Sea also contains
ny individual reefs and small islands, collectively
ed the Coral Sea Islands Territory. This sea has
pical climate, with frequent typhoons (violent
ical storms) between January and April.

AREA 1.8 million sq miles
(4.8 million sq km)

MAXIMUM DEPTH 30,070 ft (9,165 m)

INFLOWS West central Pacific Ocean;
Fly, Purari, and Kikori rivers

Southern Ocean

SOUTHERN OCEAN

ANTARCTICA

SOUTHERN OCEAN

This ocean is also known as the Antarctic Ocean because it completely surrounds Antarctica. It has the strongest winds found anywhere on the Earth. These, along with many icebergs and large waves, make ship navigation in this sea very dangerous.

AREA	7.8 million sq miles (20 million sq k
MAXIMUM DEPTH	23,735 ft (7,235 m)
INFLOWS	Summer melting of sea-ice and icebergs calved from Antarctic ice shelves

Scotia Sea

This cold sea lies between the southern Atlantic Ocean and the Southern Ocean. Icebergs from the Antarctic Ice Sheet can be found here all year round, and in the winter, sea-ice forms at the region's edges.

AREA	350,000 sq miles (900,000 sq km)
MAXIMUM DEPTH	13,000 ft (4,000 m)
INFLOWS	Southern Ocean to the west of Drake Passage

ss Sea

all the seas around Antarctica, the
ss Sea has the least sea-ice, making it very
essible to shipping. The sea is home to the
ish, which has a special protein in its body
prevents it from freezing.

EA	370,000 sq miles (960,000 sq km)
XIMUM DEPTH	8,200 ft (2,500 m)
LOWS	Icebergs calved from the ss Ice Shelf

Weddell Sea

Heavily covered in ice, this sea is home
to the Weddell seal, which swims beneath
the ice and can break through to the surface
to create breathing holes. Colonies of emperor
penguins are also found in this sea.

AREA	1.1 million sq miles (2.8 million sq km)
MAXIMUM DEPTH	10,000 ft (3,000 m)
INFLOWS	Icebergs calved from the Ronne-Filchner Ice shelf

Only five species of
bird remain on the
Scotia Sea Islands,
including the yellow-
billed pintail duck.

DISAPPEARING ISLAND
The Pacific Ocean is dotted with volcanoes that once erupted from the ocean floor but are now extinct. Bora Bora island is one of these volcanoes. As its deep source of heat cools and the rocks contract, the island is slowly sinking back beneath the waves.

The four-million-year-old
tropical island of Bora Bora

is sinking

at the rate of ½ in (1 cm)
every 100 years

What is a coral reef?

Coral reefs are wave-resistant structures made by marine creatures and their skeletons. These colorful formations are home to an incredible range of plants and animals, including sponges, worms, anemones, and mollusks such as snails, clams, and octopuses. The richest and healthiest reefs support thousands of fish and turtles.

Formation of coral reefs

Although coral reefs can be huge—stretching for up to hundreds of miles—the organisms that form them are very small. Corals are made up of tiny individual creatures called polyps. As they grow, polyps create a hard outer shell, or skeleton, of limestone. When they die, this shell remains, and new polyps grow on it. In this way, reefs are formed and continue to grow.

TYPES OF REEF

A **fringing reef** is formed as corals grow around an island or along a shoreline.

A **barrier reef** runs parallel to the shore but is separated from it by a large lagoon.

An **atoll** is a ring of coral reefs or low-lying coral islands that surrounds a shallow lagoon.

Coral damage

Today, coral reefs face many threats to their survival. Pollution and rising water temperatures can kill corals, which lose color when they die—this is known as coral bleaching. Reefs are also damaged by human activity, such as using dynamite to catch fish.

Coral bleaching

POLYPS

Corals are made up of tiny individual creatures known as polyps.

▲ Some polyps attach themselves to the seafloor or rocks using parts called basal plates.

▲ Polyps' tentacles have stinging cells, which are used to sting, paralyze, and catch prey.

▲ The tentacles surround and move food to the polyp's mouth. Its gut secretes the limestone that builds the reef.

Coral reefs

Among the Earth's most spectacular and diverse habitats, coral reefs support more species per unit of area than any other marine environment. They also protect islands and coasts from erosion.

Bahama Banks

A cluster of 700 islands make up the Bahama Banks. These islands are scattered over two limestone platforms—the Little Bahama Banks and the Great Bahama Banks. The platforms have been growing for the last 70 million years.

LOCATION	Bahamas, southeast of Florida, and northeast of Cuba
TYPE	Fringing reef, patch reef, and barrier reef
AREA	1,200 sq miles (3,150 sq km)

ghthouse Reef

coral formations of the Lighthouse
f surround a large, circular sinkhole known
he Great Blue Hole. The sinkhole is about
ft (145 m) deep and features a number of
ient stalactites hanging from its slanting walls.

ATION Western Caribbean,
iles (80 km) east of central Belize

PE Atoll with patch reef

EA 116 sq miles (300 sq km)

Aldabra Atoll

The largest raised coral atoll in the
world, Aldabra is situated on top of an ancient
volcanic peak. Strong ocean tides in Aldabra's
lagoon have turned
raised clumps of
reef into small,
mushroom-shaped
islands known as
champignons.

LOCATION Western end of the Republic of
Seychelles archipelago, northwestern Madagascar

TYPE Atoll

AREA 60 sq miles (155 sq km)

Maldives

The Maldives are a group of islands
with 26 atolls, many of which contain mini-
atolls, called faros, which are rare outside the
Maldives. Due to climate change over the past
century, the Maldives may be under threat from
rising sea levels—the highest island is
less than 10 ft (3 m) above sea level.

LOCATION Southwest of
Sri Lanka, in the Indian Ocean

TYPE Atoll and fringing reef

AREA 3,500 sq miles
(9,000 sq km)

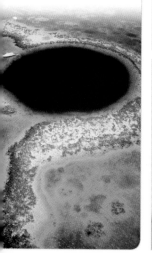

Red Sea reefs

The Red Sea contains a variety of reefs. The northern area has mostly fringing reefs, with reef flats (flat areas of reef next to the shore) only a few yards wide, while the southern Red Sea has a much wider area of shallow continental shelf—the underwater extension of a continent. The Red Sea reefs are home to a spectacular range of corals and fish, including the Red Sea lionfish.

LOCATION Red Sea coasts of Egypt, Israel, Jordan, Saudi Arabia, Sudan, Eritrea, and Yemen

TYPE Fringing reef, patch reef, and barrier reef, and atoll

AREA 6,300 sq miles (16,500 sq km)

sa Tenggara

is a chain of about 500 coral-fringed
ds. The islands in the north are volcanic
igin, while those in the south are mainly
e up of coral limestone. Nusa Tenggara
ports a huge variety of marine life—a
e large reef can contain more species
sh than all the European seas combined.

CATION Southern
nesia, from Lombok in
west to Timor in the east

E Fringing reef and
er reef

A 2,000 sq miles
0 sq km)

at Barrier Reef

Great Barrier Reef is often described
e largest structure ever made by living
nisms. It is made up of about 3,000
idual reefs and small coral islands. It
the world's largest collection of coral
, with 400 types of coral, 1,500 species
sh, and 4,000 types of mollusk.

LOCATION Parallel to Queensland
coast, northeastern Australia

TYPE Barrier reef

AREA 14,300 sq miles (37,000 sq km)

Even after a coral dies, its hard

skeleton remains

and new corals grow on it

REEF BUILDING
Many organisms, such as algae, corals, and mollusks, help
form the foundation of a coral reef. The force of the waves
and the grazing of animals help break the animal shells into
sand, which fills the gaps in the growing reef. Algae bind it
all together to form reef rock.

▲ Land-based processes include the flow of glaciers, lava, and sediment, as well as human activity.

▲ Marine-based processes include waves, tides, currents, and changing sea levels.

Coastal features

A broad area of land that borders the sea is called a coast. Coasts can feature gulfs, lagoons, dunes, and beaches. These are formed by different processes such as the flow of tides, breaking waves, or the buildup of sediments.

Oregon National Dunes

This is the largest area of coastal sand dunes in North America. The dunes were formed by a combination of erosion by sea waves, and the transport of sand by ocean winds over millions of years. Winds continue to mold the sand dunes into wavelike shapes.

LOCATION	Southwest of Portland, Oregon
TYPE	Coastal dunes
SIZE	40 miles (65 km)

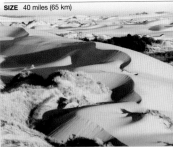

...ngeness Spit

...pit is a narrow strip of land
...nected to the coast at one end. This spit
...amed after Dungeness in England. Its
...que shape was formed by winds blowing
...n different directions in different seasons.

...CATION Seattle, Washington

...PE Sand spit

...E 5½ miles (9 km)

Gulf of Bothnia

As the surrounding land rises, the sea
level falls by about ⅓ in (7 mm) a year in this
northern arm of the Baltic Sea, revealing new
islands along the coast. The water has a low
salt content because of the large amount of
fresh water that flows into it.

LOCATION Between Finland's west coast
and Sweden's east coast

TYPE Gulf

SIZE 45,200 sq miles (117,000 sq km)

...ite Cliffs of Dover

...astal erosion by waves and tides has eaten
... the soft white limestone that forms the chalk
...fs of Dover. The chalk is made of countless
... skeletons of marine microorganisms along
...n some larger fossil shells.

LOCATION Dover, UK

TYPE Marine-based coast

SIZE 11 miles (17 km)

Durdle Door

This limestone arch used to be a cliff. Sea waves wore away the softer layers of rock at the bottom of the cliff, leaving the harder rock at the top, creating an arch.

LOCATION	Dorset, southern UK
TYPE	Arch
SIZE	200 ft (60 m) high

Skeleton Coast

This arid (dry) region has low gravel plains in the south, while in the north, sand dunes extend to the sea. Due to strong winds, the shapes of the dunes are constantly changing.

LOCATION	Northwest Windhoek, Namibia
TYPE	Marine-based coast
SIZE	310 miles (500 km)

Kerala backwaters

These slow-moving stretches of water are made up of a chain of lagoons and small lakes linked by canals. Fed by 38 rivers, the backwaters cover almost half the length of the state of Kerala.

LOCATION	Southeast Cochin, Kerala, India
TYPE	Lagoon
SIZE	400 sq miles (1,000 sq km)

Kinabatangan mangroves

The aerial, or above-ground, roots of mangrove plants trap muddy sediment to form wetland swamps. The Kinabatangan mangroves feature a range of lowland forests and open reed marsh.

LOCATION Eastern Sabah, Malaysia

TYPE Mangrove swamps

SIZE 400 sq miles (1,000 sq km)

Yangtze estuary

The longest river in Asia and its busiest waterway, the Yangtze River carries large amounts of silt and mud, which are deposited in its estuary, dividing the river into three smaller channels and many streams.

LOCATION Northwest Shanghai, China

TYPE Estuary

SIZE 1,000 sq miles (2,500 sq km)

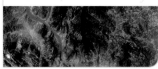

Ha Long Bay

Rising sea levels flooded an area surrounding about 2,000 karst towers, creating the karst islands that make up Ha Long Bay. Some of these islands rise to about about 650 ft (200 m) above sea level.

LOCATION Gulf of Tonkin, east Hanoi, Vietnam

TYPE Land-based coast

SIZE 75 miles (120 km)

Moeraki Beach

Moeraki Beach is famous for its large, round boulders, which are up to 10 ft (3 m) in diameter and can weigh several tons. The boulders formed as nodules in muddy sediment as it hardened into mudstone rock. The relatively soft mudstone has been worn away, leaving behind the harder boulders, which now litter the beach.

LOCATION	Northeast Dunedin, New Zealand
TYPE	Beach
SIZE	5 miles (8 km)

Ninety Mile Beach

Made up of a series of sand dunes, this is the longest natural beach in the world. Behind these dunes lie several large lakes and shallow lagoons, known as the Gippsland Lakes.

LOCATION	Southwest Melbourne, Victoria, Australia
TYPE	Beach
SIZE	94 miles (150 km)

The Twelve Apostles

When the roof of a natural rock arch erodes and collapses, it leaves behind a rock pillar called a stack. The Twelve Apostles is a group of sea stacks that were formed by the continuing wave erosion and collapse of 20-million-year-old limestone cliffs. They are still being eroded today.

LOCATION Near Port Campbell, Victoria, Australia

TYPE Marine-based coast

SIZE 2 miles (3 km)

These sea stacks are still called the Twelve Apostles, even though only eight of them remain today.

SKELETON SHIPWRECKS
On the Skeleton Coast, cold air from the Atlantic
Ocean and dry air from the Namib Desert form thick
fogs, which have often caused sailors to lose their way.
Many shipwrecks have been found here, including the
Eduard Bohlen, which was washed ashore in 1909.

The Skeleton Coast is called
"the land God made in anger,"
because of its harsh climate and dense ocean fog that has caused many shipwrecks

Atmosphere

layer of gases, called the atmosphere, surrounds
e Earth. The Sun's rays pass through the atmosphere,
arming the Earth's surface and the air above it, causing
e air to move and water to evaporate. This results in
ifferent weather conditions. Changes in weather can
so be caused by land-based events, such as the
olcanic eruptions at Eyjafjallajökull, Iceland, in 2010,
hich created a huge ash cloud.

DESTRUCTIVE WHIRL
Swirling winds over
warm ocean waters lead
to hurricanes. In 2011,
Hurricane Irene hit the
US, the Atlantic coast of
Canada, and the Caribbean.

The Earth's atmosphere

The Earth is surrounded by a blanket of gases called the atmosphere, which is made up mainly of nitrogen and oxygen with tiny amounts of water vapor and other gases. The atmosphere is at its most dense near the Earth's surface. As altitude increases, it gets thinner, eventually fading into space.

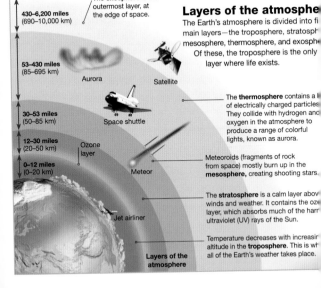

The **exosphere** is the outermost layer, at the edge of space.

430–6,200 miles
(690–10,000 km)

53–430 miles
(85–695 km)

Aurora

Satellite

30–53 miles
(50–85 km)

Space shuttle

12–30 miles
(20–50 km)

Ozone layer

0–12 miles
(0–20 km)

Meteor

Jet airliner

Layers of the atmosphere

Layers of the atmosphe[re]

The Earth's atmosphere is divided into fi[ve] main layers—the troposphere, stratosph[ere] mesosphere, thermosphere, and exosph[ere] Of these, the troposphere is the only layer where life exists.

The **thermosphere** contains a l[ayer] of electrically charged particles They collide with hydrogen and oxygen in the atmosphere to produce a range of colorful lights, known as aurora.

Meteoroids (fragments of rock from space) mostly burn up in the **mesosphere,** creating shooting stars.

The **stratosphere** is a calm layer abov[e] winds and weather. It contains the ozo[ne] layer, which absorbs much of the harm[ful] ultraviolet (UV) rays of the Sun.

Temperature decreases with increasin[g] altitude in the **troposphere**. This is wh[ere] all of the Earth's weather takes place.

Water and the atmosphere

The movement of water between the atmosphere, the land, and the Earth's oceans, lakes, and rivers is called the water cycle. The Sun's heat causes the Earth's liquid water to evaporate, or turn into water vapor. This water vapor rises and collects to form clouds. Water falls back to land and eventually returns to the oceans and lakes.

Clouds carry water to land in the form of **rain and snow**

Water **evaporates** from sea

Vapor cools to form **clouds**

...er seeps **ground**

Water returns to sea via **rivers and streams**

Water cycle

Jet streams

Jet streams are long, narrow bands of high-speed winds in the upper troposphere or lower stratosphere. The wind here is so strong that pilots can cut hours off their flight time by flying along these jet streams. Hot air from the aircraft engines condenses to form long, thin clouds of water vapor, known as contrails.

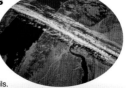

Contrails above the Red Sea

Precipitation

When air cools, water vapor condenses—turns from gas into liquid—forming clouds. When cloud particles become too heavy to remain suspended in the air, they fall to the Earth as precipitation. This may be in the form of rain, snow, dew, fog, or hail.

Dew

Dew forms overnight when warm, moist air rising from the ground meets cold nigh causing the rising moisture to condense on the ground as droplets of water.

CLOUD	None
INTENSITY	Light to heavy

Rain

Rain is liquid precipitation th falls in drops. These vary in s from tiny drizzle as small as $1/50$ in ($1/2$ mm) wide to drops up to $1/4$ in (6 mm) wide. Mos raindrops are $2/25$–$1/5$ in (2–5 mm) in diameter.

CLOUD	Nimbostratus–cumulonimbus
INTENSITY	Light to heavy

...og, or haar, is formed when warm
...air comes into contact with cold
...ater and the moisture condenses
...y droplets.

CLOUD Low-level stratus

INTENSITY Light to dense

...ones are lumps of ice that form
...rozen drops of rain, kept in the air by
... winds, get blown around in freezing
...erclouds until they are heavy enough
...to the Earth. They may be smaller
...eas or as big as oranges.

...D Tall cumulus

...SITY

...o heavy

Snow

When tiny ice crystals in clouds stick together,
they form snowflakes. When they become heavy
enough, they fall to the ground as snow. Snowfall
is heaviest when temperatures are around freezing
point, which is 32° F (0° C).

CLOUD Cumulus and stratus

INTENSITY Light to heavy

Cloud types

Clouds consist of ice crystals or water droplets. According to the height of their base above the ground, they are identified as high, middle, or low. Cloud types are defined by air temperature and the amount of water in the cloud.

FOCUS ON...
LIGHTNING
Electrical charges within clouds bui and result in light seen in various sl and forms in the

Cirrus

High, wispy clouds shaped like long streamers are called cirrus clouds or horse tails. These clouds are made up of ice crystals because they form in extremely cold parts of the atmosphere. Cirrus clouds are a sign of fair and pleasant weather.

ALTITUDE 18,000–40,000 ft (5,500–12,000 m)

SHAPE Layered, tufted, or patchy

PRECIPITATION None

Cirrocumulus

These rounded, white puffs are usually see in long rows. They have ripples that resem a honeycomb or the scales of a fish. Usua seen in the winter, they indicate fair but cold weather.

ALTITUDE 20,000–40,000 ft (6,000–12,000 m)

SHAPE Layers or patches of cells

PRECIPITATION None

▲ ...ud-to-ground ...ng strikes ...ound from a ...onimbus cloud.

▲ Ground-to-cloud lightning moves from the ground to a cumulonimbus cloud.

▲ Cloud-to-cloud lightning occurs between different clouds, without touching the ground.

▲ Ball lightning is a bright ball that may occur with cloud-to-ground lightning.

...ostratus

...e thin, high, sheetlike clouds
... the entire sky, making it look milky.
... are not thick enough to hide the Sun
...Moon completely, but can produce a halo
...nd them. They usually form 12–24 hours
...e a rain or snow storm.

...UDE	18,000–40,000 ft (5,500–12,000 m)
...E	Layered
...IPITATION	None

Altocumulus

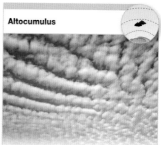

Altocumulus clouds look like rolls. These may be arranged in lines, waves, or round masses. When altocumulus forms with "towers" billowing upward, it warns of approaching heavy showers and possible thunderstorms.

ALTITUDE	6,500–18,000 ft (2,000–5,500 m)
SHAPE	Parallel bands or rounded masses
PRECIPITATION	Possible thunderstorms or showers

Altostratus

These clouds contain ice crystals near the top and water droplets lower down. Altostratus clouds can cover the entire sky in such a way that the Sun and Moon are faintly visible through them. These clouds may produce light snow or rain.

ALTITUDE 6,500–18,000 ft (2,000–5,500 m)

SHAPE Layered and featureless

PRECIPITATION Almost none

Stratocumulus

These low, puffy gray or white clouds are seen in rows, lines, or waves separated by patches of blue sky. They may appear in many weather conditions and can produce light rain or snow.

ALTITUDE 1,150–6,500 ft (350–2,000 m)

SHAPE Large and rounded

PRECIPITATION Light

...atus

...tly featureless, these uniform gray or white
...ds cover the sky in a blanket. They can form
...er thick enough to completely block out the
...or Moon. They often form overnight in fine
...her, especially over the sea.

ALTITUDE 0–6,500 ft (0–2,000 m)

SHAPE Layered

PRECIPITATION Light

...mulus

...se individual, puffy clouds look like cotton
...s floating in the sky. Cumulus clouds are flat
...e base and have rounded tops that often
...like cauliflower heads. They appear very
...e, with clearly defined edges.

ALTITUDE 0–6,500 ft (0–2,000 m)

SHAPE Cauliflower or fluffy

PRECIPITATION Occasional rain
or snow showers

Cumulonimbus

When cumulus clouds grow taller, they form
giant cumulonimbus clouds. High winds flatten
the tops of these thunderstorm clouds into the
shape of an anvil, which points in the direction
the storm is moving. These clouds produce
heavy rain or snow, as well as hailstorms
and tornadoes.

ALTITUDE	1,000–6,500 ft (300–2,000 m)
SHAPE	Stringy upper edges and anvil top
PRECIPITATION	Heavy rain and thunderstorms

Nimbostratus

n altostratus clouds thicken, they
elop into nimbostratus clouds. These
shapeless and dark, but may appear
from inside because of gaps in them.
se clouds are so thick, they can hide
Sun and the Moon completely, resulting
ull days and dark nights.

TUDE 2,000–10,000 ft (600–3,000 m)

PE Layered and featureless

CIPITATION Continuous rain or snow likely

Lenticular clouds

These disk-shaped clouds form when
the wind blows from the same direction at
different levels of the troposphere. Usually seen
in mountains or hilly areas, lenticular clouds are
sometimes described as a "stack of pancakes."

ALTITUDE	6,500–16,400 ft (2,000–5,000 m)
SHAPE	Lens-shaped or saucerlike
PRECIPITATION	Possible light rain or snow

In 1959, William Rankin, a US Air Force pilot, had to eject from his burning aircraft and became the first person to survive a fall through a cumulonimbus cloud, after being **trapped inside it** for half an hour due to upward air currents

CLOUDS OF DANGER
Unlike other clouds, cumulonimbus clouds may release all their moisture at once, resulting in lightning, severe hailstorms, thunderstorms, and even tornadoes. This makes these clouds especially dangerous for planes to fly through.

Storms

A storm is a powerful disturbance in the atmosphere. It typically features strong winds, cloudy skies, and heavy precipitation. Violent storms produce strong, fast winds such as tornadoes (narrow funnels of rapidly spinning air), cyclones (warm winds rising in a spiral), and hurricanes (tropical cyclones).

Storm of the Century

This week-long storm was accompanied by heavy snow, tornadoes, and freezing temperatures. Severe snowstorms, called blizzards, caused major damage to power lines, leading to power failures that affected more than 10 million people.

LOCATION	US and Canada
YEAR	1993
TYPE	Snowstorm

Oklahoma Tornado Outbreak

Situated in a tornado-prone area, the state of Oklahoma experiences several hundred tornadoes every year. On May 1999, more than 70 tornadoes struck the state causing widespread destruction—demolishing thousands of homes and whipping up huge clouds of debris. The storms lasted for three days and caused damage worth a billion dollar

LOCATION	Oklahoma
YEAR	1999
TYPE	Tornado

rricane Katrina

of the five deadliest hurricanes to hit the US, icane Katrina killed more than 1,800 people caused damage worth 90 billion dollars. In Orleans, high waves and torrential rains led idespread flooding. About 80 percent of the was flooded up to a depth of 23 ft (7 m).

LOCATION	New Orleans, Louisiana
YEAR	2005
TYPE	Hurricane

eat Ice Storm

ombination of five smaller ice storms, this rm resulted in more than 80 hours of freezing . Layers of ice built up, damaging trees and ging down power lines. This caused massive er failures, with some areas remaining out power for weeks.

LOCATION	Canada and US
YEAR	1998
TYPE	Ice storm

Cyclone Nargis

The deadliest cyclone ever recorded in this region, Nargis caused massive damage and many deaths, both during the storm and after it ended. Several thousand people drowned, while others died of diseases caused by rotting bodies, dirty floodwater, and mosquitoes.

LOCATION Myanmar

YEAR 2008

TYPE Cyclone

Chinese Dust Storm

Dust and sand storms occur in arid or semiarid areas where there aren't enough trees hold the soil in place and it gets whipped up i the air by the wind. This dust storm from the G Desert covered 313,000 sq miles (810,000 sq k

LOCATION China

YEAR 2010

TYPE Dust storm

Red Dust Storm

A cloud of red-orange dust, more than 600 miles (1,000 km) long, spread from Australia's deserts and dry farmland to Sydney and the eastern coast of Australia. This storm caused major disruption to international flights

LOCATION Eastern coast of Australia

YEAR 2009

TYPE Dust storm

ack Saturday Bushfires

The heat from the wildfire was powerful enough to kill anyone within 1,000 ft (300 m).

en lightning strikes dry vegetation, it
cause a fire. This wildfire started as
e small fires. High-speed winds of up to
mph (90 kph) rapidly spread the fires,
sing massive damage.

LOCATION	Victoria, Australia
YEAR	2009
TYPE	Wildfire

In 1931, a powerful tornado in Mississippi

lifted a train

weighing 91 tons (83 metric tonnes)
up into the air and tossed it 80 ft
(24 m) away from the track

TORNADO FORCE
A tornado, or twister, is a storm in
which a column of air, usually about
328 ft (100 m) wide, spins violently. It can
completely destroy an area, uprooting trees,
overturning cars, and wrecking buildings.

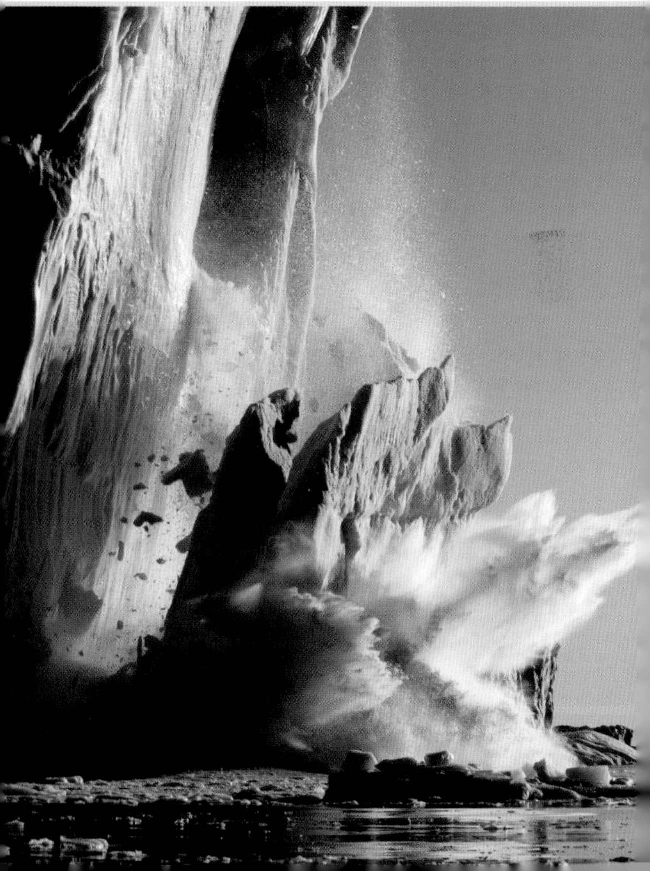

Climate

The weather changes every day, with variations in temperature, precipitation, wind, and clouds. When the weather is examined over several years, a pattern emerges. This pattern, repeated over many years, is known as the climate of a particular region. Scientists divide the world into regions according to their climates. These regions range from icy polar zones to hot tropical areas.

GLOBAL WARMING
At present, the average global temperature is rising, but this rise is not spread evenly around the Earth. Some areas are getting warmer, while others are getting colder.

Global warming

Global warming is the term given to the rise in the Earth's average temperature. Climate change is a natural process and has been going on for billions of years. However, human activity has recently caused the rate of change to increase, which is causing many serious environmental problems.

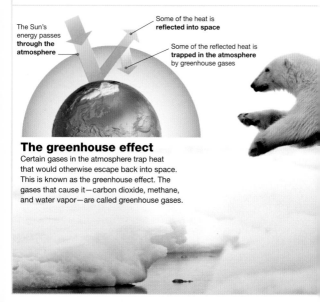

The Sun's energy passes **through the atmosphere**

Some of the heat is **reflected into space**

Some of the reflected heat is **trapped in the atmosphere** by greenhouse gases

The greenhouse effect

Certain gases in the atmosphere trap heat that would otherwise escape back into space. This is known as the greenhouse effect. The gases that cause it—carbon dioxide, methane, and water vapor—are called greenhouse gases.

Causes of global warming

Greenhouse gases, which increase the greenhouse effect, are released into the atmosphere by aircraft and car exhausts, as well as when fossil fuels are burned in factories and power plants. Greenhouse gases are also found in aerosols and old refrigerators.

ects of global warming

e from changing weather patterns requent storms, the high rate of global ling causes glaciers and polar ice to melt. may lead to a rise in sea levels, flooding -lying areas. This can threaten plants and nimals that may not be able to adapt quickly enough to the change, such as polar bears. Ice is vital for them— they use it as a bridge to move across the ocean to hunt for food. If this ice melts, these bears may not survive.

Helping the planet

To try to stop global warming, the release of greenhouse gases into the atmosphere from factories, cars, and other sources will have to be reduced. The use of "cleaner," renewable energy sources, such as solar and wind power, will help, as will the recycling of materials (such as paper), environmentally friendly transportation (such as cycling), and the replanting of forests.

Climate regions

The climate of a region determines its main characteristics—temperature, rainfall, soil type, and plant growth. Based on these, regions are identified and classified into different biomes, or climate regions.

FOCUS ON...
FACTORS
Many factors are responsible for the variations in climate around the world.

Temperate

Temperate areas have varied climates, but the average monthly temperature ranges between 64°F (18°C) and 27°F (-3°C). In the warmest month, the average temperature is above 50°F (10°C). These regions have four distinct seasons, but can experience unpredictable weather throughout the year.

DISTRIBUTION Most regions lying between the tropical and polar regions

TYPICAL LOCATION Cork, Ireland, where temperature ranges from 48°F (9°C) to 68°F (20°C)

Tropical

Humid, tropical climates have a high annual rainfall and an average yearly temperature of at least 64°F (18°C). More than half the world's species of plant are found in these regions, which typically feature a dense tree cover.

▲ Oceans absorb and transport heat from the Sun, giving coastal regions a moderate climate.

▲ Temperature decreases at higher altitudes, making mountains colder than lower-lying areas.

…reas close to the …uator are hotter as … Sun's rays fall directly …these regions.

…TRIBUTION Most regions along …equator

…PICAL LOCATION Dodoma, Tanzania, …re temperature ranges from 79°F (26°C) …88°F (31°C)

Mountain

Although temperature decreases with height everywhere, the climate of each mountain varies according to the region in which it is located. For example, those parts of the Andes that lie in Colombia receive frequent rainfall, but parts that lie in Ecuador are usually dry.

DISTRIBUTION Mountains, plateaus, and ranges, about 2,000 ft (600 m) above sea level

TYPICAL LOCATION Les Escaldes, Andorra, where temperature ranges from 43°F (6°C) to 79°F (26°C)

Polar

The Arctic and Antarctic regions, located at the Earth's North and South poles, have an extremely cold and dry climate. All precipitation falls as snow, which remains on the ground and builds up gradually over time.

DISTRIBUTION Arctic and Antarctic circles

TYPICAL LOCATION Vostok Station, Antarctica, where the temperature ranges from -89°F (-67°C) to -26°F (-32°C)

Mediterranean

Regions with mild, wet winters and warm, dry summers are said to have a Mediterranean climate. Rainfall averages 15 in (380 mm) a year, falling mainly between December and March, with usually no rain at all in August.

DISTRIBUTION Southern Europe, South Africa, and southern Australia

TYPICAL LOCATION Rome, Italy, where the temperature ranges from 52°F (11°C) to 86°F (30°C)

areas are hot and dry, with high levels of
poration and low precipitation. They include
deserts such as the Sahara, which receives
ain for years, and semidesert areas such
e Sahel, which has a short rainy season.

DISTRIBUTION Most deserts

TYPICAL LOCATION I-n-Salah, Algeria,
where the temperature ranges from 70°F (21°C)
to 113°F (45°C).

Did you know?

EARTH STATISTICS

★ The Earth is **4.6 billion years old.**

★ The first appearance of life on the Earth occurred at least **3.4 billion years ago,** as shown by fossils of microbes found in Australia.

★ The Earth's diameter at the equator is **7,926 miles (12,756 km).**

★ The Earth measures **24,900 miles (40,075 km)** around the equator.

★ The average distance of the Earth from the Sun is **93 million miles (149.6 million km).**

★ The average distance that the Earth's tectonic plates move in one year is **4½ in (11 cm).**

★ The depth of the troposphere varies between **5 and 11 miles (8 and 18 km).**

★ The Earth orbits the Sun at a speed of **67,000 mph (107,300 kph).**

★ The Earth rotates at **994 mph (1,600 kph),** completing one spin every 24 hours.

★ The Earth spins on an axis that is at present tilted **23.5°** from the vertical. Th tilt means that different amounts of sunl reach the Earth's surface as it orbits the over a year, resulting in the seasons.

★ It takes **8.3 minutes** for light from the Sun to reach the Earth.

★ The Earth's average surface tempera is **59°F (15°C).**

DISCOVERY AND INVENTI

The following are some of the most important Earth-related scientific discoveries and inventions from the past few thousand years.

▶ **c.280** BCE
Greek astronomer Aristarchus is the first to estimate the **distance betwee the Earth and the Sun.** He also sugg that the planet Earth rotates on its axis and revolves around the Sun, although few people believe him at this time.

▶ **23** CE
Greek geographer and historian Strabo states that **earthquakes and volcanoes** cause land to rise and sink.

▶ **100**

hinese invent the **magnetic compass.**
s a pivoting magnetized needle to point
Earth's poles.

▶ **19–21**

guese navigator Ferdinand Magellan
ut on the **first sailing expedition
nd the world.** He is killed in the
pines, but the surviving sailors
lete the voyage.

▶ **43**

n astronomer Nicolaus Copernicus
s that the **planets orbit the Sun
that the Earth spins on its axis.**
this time, most people believed that the
lay at the center of the universe.

▶ **09**

astronomer and mathematician
o Galilei uses a telescope to produce
st scientific proof for Copernicus's theory
t the **movement of the planets.**

▶ **69**

sh scholar Nicolaus Steno describes
rinciples of stratigraphy. This says
ayers of rock, or strata, are deposited
on top of the other, with the youngest
a being on top.

▶ **'98**

sh physicist Henry Cavendish determines
mass and density of the Earth.

▶ **1824**
William Buckland of the University of Oxford
writes the **first scientific paper about a
dinosaur,** pioneering the use of fossils to
reconstruct the Earth's timeline.

▶ **1827**
French mathematician Jean Baptiste
Fourier introduces the concept of the
greenhouse effect.

▶ **1880**
English geologist John Milne invents the
modern seismograph (an instrument
for measuring earthquakes).

▶ **1895**
Swedish chemist Svante Arrhenius
suggests that carbon dioxide added to the
Earth's atmosphere helps trap heat from
the Sun, leading to **global warming.**

▶ **1912**
German meteorologist Alfred Wegener
proposes the theory of **continental drift.**
He claims that about 270 mya a giant
landmass, the supercontinent of Pangaea,
broke up into smaller pieces, leading to the
continents we recognize today.

▶ **1953**
US scientist Claire Patterson first
accurately **estimates the Earth's age**
by comparing measurements taken
from meteorites and minerals.

Amazing Earth facts

HIGHEST MOUNTAINS

❶ **Mount Everest,** in the Himalayas, is the Earth's highest mountain, at 29,035 ft (8,850 m) above sea level.

❷ **K2** is part of the northwestern region of the Karakoram Range. This peak stands at a height of 28,250 ft (8,611 m) above sea level.

❸ **Kanchenjunga** means "the five treasures of snows." It is named for its five peaks, of which the highest is 28,169 ft (8,586 m) above sea level.

❹ **Lhotse** is 27,940 ft (8,516 m) above sea level. It is found on the border between Tibet and the Khumbu region of Nepal.

❺ **Makalu,** in the Himalayas, is an isolated peak shaped like a four-sided pyramid. It is 27,766 ft (8,463 m) high.

❻ **Cho Oyu** is 26,906 ft (8,201 m) above sea level. It lies in the Himalayas and is 12²/₅ miles (20 km) west of Mount Everest, on the border between China and Nepal.

Measured from its oceanic base, Mauna Kea in Hawaii is more than 33,465 ft (10,200 m) high—even taller than Mount Everest.

❼ **Dhaulagiri** is 26,795 ft (8,167 m) hig Its name means "pure white mountain."

❽ **Manaslu** is 26,781 ft (8,163 m) above sea level and is a part of the Nepalese Himalayas, in the west-central part of Nepal. Manaslu is also known as Kutang.

❾ **Nanga Parbat** is known in Kas India, as Diamir, which means " of the mountains." It rises to height of 26,657 ft (8,125 n

❿ **Annapurna** is a sectio the Himalayas in north-cer Nepal. Its highest peak is 26,542 ft (8,090 m) high.

DEADLIEST ERUPTION

❶ In 1815, the **Tambora volcano** erup in Indonesia, sending dust clouds aroun globe and dimming the sun. Around 70,0 people were killed from the eruption and after effects, such as famine and disease

❷ The **Krakatau volcano** exploded in 1883, killing around 36,000 people. This explosion is believed to be the loudest sound recorded in recent history.

1902, the town of St. Pierre, on
Caribbean island of Martinique, was
royed by burning clouds of dust from
nt Pelée. This eruption killed more
29,000 people.

1985, the eruption of the **Ruiz
ano,** in Colombia, caused a massive
flow, which engulfed the town of
ero, 37 miles (60 km) away. More than
00 people were buried in the mud.

ount Unzen is an active group
everal overlapping stratovolcanoes
pan. In 1792, the collapse of one
lava domes triggered a tsunami
killed about 15,000 people.

1783, **Laki Mountain,** in
nd, poured out lava and gases,
h spread as far as Europe and
America. Around 9,500 people
killed in Iceland alone.

he eruption of **Santa Maria**
uatemala, in 1902, was one of
argest volcanic eruptions of the
century. Around 6,000 people
killed.

elud, a volcano in Indonesia, is known
arge, explosive eruptions. More than
ruptions have occurred since 1000 CE.
919, an eruption at Kelud killed an
nated 5,000 people.

❾ Galunggung is an active stratovolcano
in west Java, Indonesia. In 1822, an
eruption killed more than 4,000 people.

❿ Mount Vesuvius is a stratovolcano in
the Gulf of Naples, Italy. Since the famous
eruption of 79 CE, which destroyed the city
of Pompeii and the town of Herculaneum,
it has erupted many times.

DEEPEST OCEANIC TRENCHES

❶ At a depth of 35,794 ft (10,910 m),
the **Mariana Trench** in the Pacific Ocean
is the deepest spot in the world's oceans.

❷ Located in the southern Pacific
Ocean, the **Tonga Trench** is up to
35,700 ft (10,880 m) deep.

❸ The **Kuril–Kamchatka Trench** or
Kuril Trench is located in the northwestern
part of the Pacific Ocean. It is 34,587 ft
(10,542 m) deep.

❹ The **Philippines Trench** is a
submarine trench that lies to the east of the
Philippines. It is 34,580 ft (10,540 m) deep.

❺ The **Kermadec Trench,** which is
32,972 ft (10,050 m) deep, was formed
by the subduction of the Pacific Plate
under the Indo-Australian Plate.

Glossary

Algae A diverse group of simple plantlike organisms, the largest of which are seaweeds.

Arid A weather condition that is very dry and supports little plant and animal life.

Aurora Bands of colored light in the sky over the North and South poles.

Basaltic lava The hottest type of lava, with the lowest silica content. It is runnier than other lavas and cools to form basalt.

Basin A depression on the Earth's surface filled with water, from where a river and all its branches and tributaries drain.

Batholith A huge mass of igneous rock that often forms the core of mountains.

Beach An area of land marking the margin of a coastline. It usually consists of loose rock particles, such as sand, gravel, or pebbles.

Biome A region of the Earth that has a particular type of climate, soil, and plant and animal life.

Blizzard A storm in which thick snow falls fast and hard.

Boreal An ecosystem or habitat of or related to sub-Arctic areas, usually used to describe forests of that region.

Caldera A crater, or depression, at the top of a volcano. It forms when the peak collapses into the volcano's magma chamber.

Condensation The change of water vapor into liquid water.

Coniferous forest A biome that is made up of coniferous trees. It has cold, snowy winters and warm, humid summers.

Cyclone A storm in which warm, moist winds rise in a spiral. A tropical cyclone is also called a hurricane.

Delta The sediment deposited at the mouth of a river. It usually forms a triangular shape.

Drizzle Small droplets of liquid precipitation, formed in a low-layer cloud.

Dyke A thin, sheetlike body of igneous rock that cuts into older rocks.

Environment The physical features of an area, including air, water, and soil.

Equator An imaginary line around the middle of the Earth. It is at an equal distance from both poles.

Erosion The wearing away of soil and rock by wind, gravity, water, or ice.

Estuary A type of wetland where fresh water mixes with seawater at the mouth of a river.

Evaporation The change of liquid water into water vapor.

Fjord A valley that has been deepened by a glacier and then filled with seawater.

Fog A thick cloud that forms at or near the Earth's surface.

Fossil The remains or impression of an organism preserved in rock.

Fossil fuel A carbon compound, such as coal or natural gas, formed over millions of years, from the compressed, decayed remains of dead organisms. It is burned to release energy.

Fumarole A volcanic vent or opening that emits gases.

Geyser A spring that releases boiling water steam from the grou is formed when grou water is heated up b magma inside the Ea

Gorge A narrow, dee valley, usually with ve cliffs on each side.

Ground water Underground water, in gaps in soil or rock

Habitat The environment in which an organism lives.

Hemisphere The ter used to describe the northern and southe halves of the Earth a divided by the equat

Hurricane A powerfu storm that blows ove tropical oceans. In m parts of the world, a hurricane is known a a typhoon or cyclone

Icecap A mass of permanent ice coveri a large area, especia in polar regions.

Ice sheet A layer of permanent ice coveri a vast area of land.

Ice shelf An ice shee extending into the oc

Karst A landscape formed by the dissolu of rock, usually limes by water. Karsts often feature large network of caves.

n An area of
sea that is
...ted from the main
...sand or a reef.

...Molten rock that
...pted onto the
... of the Earth from
...ithin the crust.

...g A discharge of
...city in the sky.

... Molten rock
... deep within
...th.

... chamber An
...eneath a volcano
...magma builds up
... an eruption.

... A type of low-
...etland that is
...ly covered with
...nd reeds.

...ean ridge
...erwater volcanic
...ain range formed
...ectonic plates part
...va erupts through
... to form a new
...floor.

...tion A regular
..., usually seasonal,
...by an animal in
... of food, water,
...d breeding
...ons.

...al A natural
...cal substance that
... up rocks.

... The path on
...a planet travels
... the Sun, or a moon
... around a planet.

Organic Anything
that is living or has
been formed by a
living organism.

Peninsula A body of land
that is surrounded by
water on three sides.

Permafrost Soil that
remains frozen for at
least two years. It occurs
mainly in polar regions.

Plankton Tiny living
organisms that float or
drift near the surface of
the sea.

Plateau A large area
of flat land that stands
above its surroundings.

Rift A widening, valleylike
crack in the Earth's crust.

Salinity The saltiness
of a substance—for
example, water.

Savanna An area of
grassland with very
few trees that occurs
at the edge of the tropics.

Sediments Particles
of rock, mineral, or
organic matter that
are carried by wind,
water, and ice. The
deposition of these
particles is called
sedimentation.

Sill An igneous rock
formation that occurs
as a flat layer. It is
formed when magma
is squeezed between
layers of existing rocks.

Stalactite An icicle-
shaped mineral deposit
that hangs from
the roof of a cave.

Stalagmite An
icicle-shaped mineral
deposit that builds up
from the floor of a cave.

Storm A violent
disturbance in the Earth's
atmosphere. It is usually
accompanied by strong
winds and heavy
precipitation.

Subduction The
term used to describe
the movement of one
tectonic plate beneath
another. Subduction often
occurs at convergent
boundaries.

Supercontinent
An enormous landmass
consisting of several
continental plates.

Temperate Of or relating
to biomes with cool,
varied climate throughout
the year.

Temperature The
degree or intensity of
heat present in an object
or organism.

Thunder The sound
produced by the instant,
intense heating and
expansion of air by
lightning.

Tornado A violent and
destructive storm with a
funnel cloud and strong,
spinning winds.

Tropical Of or
relating to biomes
that have a hot,
humid climate with
plenty of rainfall.

Tsunami A massive,
often destructive wave,
caused by earthquakes
or volcanic eruptions.

Ultraviolet (UV) rays
Certain rays of the Sun
that can be harmful.

Volcanic plug A core
of solidified molten rock
that blocks the neck of
a volcano.

Volcano A vent in the
Earth's crust through
which magma erupts,
as well as the structure
created by this eruption.

Water vapor The
gaseous form of water.

Index

Acknowledgments

Dorling Kindersley would like to thank:
Caitlin Doyle for proofreading and Helen Peters
for indexing.

The publisher would like to thank the following
for their kind permission to reproduce
their photographs:

(Key: a-above; b-below/bottom; c-center; f-far; l-left;
r-right; t-top)

1 NASA: Visible Earth / Reto Stockli / Alan Nelson /
Fritz Hasler (bl). 2-3 Getty Images: Ron Dahlquist /
Perspectives (c). 4-5 Science Photo Library: Mark
Garlick (b). 5 Dreamstime.com: Brett Critchley (crb).
NASA: Visible Earth / Reto Stockli / Alan Nelson / Fritz
Hasler (fr / Earth); JPL (tc, tl, tl / Uranus, tc / Mars, tr /
Venus); Hubble Space Telescope Collection (tr /
Mercury, tc / Jupiter). 6 Corbis: Reg Morrison / Auscape
/ Minden Pictures (c). 6-7 Dorling Kindersley: Peter
Minister, Digital Sculptor (tc). 7 Getty Images:
Encyclopaedia Britannica / UIG (cr); Max Dannenbaum /
Stone (br). 8-9 Dorling Kindersley: Satellite ImageMap
Copyright (c) 1996-2003 Planetary Visions (c). 9
Dreamstime.com: Keith Wheatley (br). Shutterstock:
(c). 12 Corbis: Lloyd Cluff (b). 13 Corbis: Xinhua /
XINHUA (tr). NASA: (crb); JSC Digital Image Collection
(b). 14-15 Getty Images: Carsten Peter / Speleoresearch
and Films / National Geographic. 16 Corbis: George
Steinmetz. 17 Getty Images: Sami Sarkis /
Photographer's Choice RF (bc). 18 Dreamstime.com:
Yarek Gora (crb); Stephan Pietzko (c). 19 Courtesy of
the National Science Foundation: Peter Rejcek (tl).
Shutterstock: Joe Belanger (b). 20 Dreamstime.com: Mike
Brake (bl); Steve Estvanik (br). 21 Corbis: Momatiuk—
Eastcott (tr). Dreamstime.com: Sergeytoronto (b). 22
Dreamstime.com: Ama22 (tl). 22-23 Corbis: Yann
Arthus-Bertrand (bc); Kay Nietfeld / dpa (tc). 23 Getty
Images: LatitudeStock—David Forman / Gallo Images
(b). 24 Corbis: Myung Jo Lee / Alfo Relax (t); Nigel
Pavitt / JAI (br). 25 Corbis: Galen Rowell (b).
Dreamstime.com: Blagov58 (t). 26 Dreamstime.
com: Leonid Spektor (b). 26-27 Dreamstime.com: Roger
Ressmeyer (bc). 27 Alamy Images: FLPA (br). Corbis:
Richard Roscoe / Stocktrek Images (t); Luther Slabon /
Epa (tr). 28 Corbis: Vittoriano Rastelli (b). 28-29
Corbis: Kazuyoshi Nomachi (c). 29 Corbis: George
Steinmetz (br). Dreamstime.com: Craig Hanson (cr).
30-31 Corbis: Alberto Garcia. 32 Dreamstime.com:
Derekteo (b). 33 Corbis: Roger Ressmeyer (tr); Ralph
White (tr). Dorling Kindersley: Natural History Museum,
London (b). Dreamstime.com: Adreslebedev (c);
Miloslav Doubrava (br). 34 Dreamstime.com:
Dariophotography (c). 34-35 Dreamstime.com:
Piter99 (c). 35 Corbis: Yann Arthus-Bertrand (c).
Dreamstime.com: Svrid36 (b). 39 Alamy Images:
WildStock (t). 41 Dreamstime.com: Victorua (br).
Getty Images: Olivier Goujon / Robert Harding World
Imagery (t). 42 Corbis: NASA (bl). 42-43 Dreamstime.
com: Ewamewa2 (bc). Getty Images: Robert Caputo /
Aurora (t). 43 Alamy Images: Bill Bachman (br). Corbis:
Martin Harvey (t). 44-45 Dreamstime.com: Chun
Guo. 46 Dreamstime.com: Giovanni Gagliardi (b).
46-47 Corbis: Adam Woolfitt (t). 47 Alamy Images:
Olivier Parent (t). Corbis: Frans Lanting (b). 48 Corbis:
Marilyn Angel Wynn / Nativestock (tr); David
Prichard / First Light (c). 49 Corbis: Scott T. Smith (t).

Dreamstime.com: Meandr (b). 50 Dreamstime.com:
Dshamanov (b). 50-51 Dreamstime.com: Alexandr
Malyshev (tc); Witr (bc). 51 Dreamstime.com:
Marshall Space Flight Center / Nasa (br). 52 Corbis:
Sean Russell / fstop (b). 53 Alamy Images: Juergen
Richter (b). Getty Images: Randy Wells / Stone (tr). 54
(c). 55 Alamy Images: Kazuyoshi Nomachi (br). Dreamstime.com:
Lagartija (br). Getty Images: Natphotos / Digital Vision
(t). 55 Alamy Images: Images and Stories (t). Getty
Images: Peter Walton Photography / Photolibrary (b).
56 NASA: (bl). 56-57 Dreamstime.com: Maxfx (tc).
Corbis: James Balog / Aurora Photos (bc). 57 Corbis:
Frank Krahmer (br). Dreamstime.com: Ihervas (cr).
58-59 Getty Images: moodboard / the Agency
Collection. 60 Alamy Images: Chris Mattison (cl).
Tony Waltham Geophotos: (br). 61 Getty Images:
Joe Cornish / The Image Bank (t). SuperStock:
imagebroker.net (br). Tony Waltham Geophotos: (clb).
62 Corbis: Momatiuk—Eastcott (b). Dreamstime.com:
Attila Tatár (br). 63 Corbis: Peter Johnson (br).
Dreamstime.com: Genghiscat (tl). Getty Images: Cris
Bouroncle / Afp (tc); Darla Delimont / Gallo Images (tr).
Frans Lemmens / Stone (cl). 64 Corbis: Paul Souders (t);
George Steinmetz (b). 65 Getty Images: Ted Mead /
Photolibrary (t, b). 66-67 Corbis: Ed Darack / Science
Faction. 68 Alamy Images: Ange / Melissnet, D
(c). Shutterstock: Yuriy Kulyk (cl). 69 Corbis: Jim
Brandenburg / Minden Pictures (cl); Jochen Schlenker /
Westend61 (cr). Frans Lanting (b). 70 Corbis: Adrian
Arbib (bl). Getty Images: Tim Graham (t). 70-71
Dreamstime.com: Steffen Foerster (bc). 71 Corbis:
Frans Lanting (b). 72 Corbis: Ocean. 73 Getty Images:
Ted Mead / Photolibrary (br); Peter Walton Photography /
Photolibrary (t). 74 Getty Images: DEA / P. Jaccod (br);
Zack Seckler / The Image Bank (bl). 75 Corbis: Haiku
Expressed / First Light (t); cry Waltham / Robert
Harding World Imagery (br); Image Source (cr). 76
Corbis: Alaska Stock (b). 77 Corbis: Jenny E. Ross.
78-79 Getty Images: Robert Postma / First Light. 80
Alamy Images: Bill Bachman (cr). Dreamstime.com:
Bondarenko Olesya (b). 81 Dreamstime.com: Ina Van
Hateren (cl); Ivan Kok Cheong Hor (cr). Getty Images:
Peter Walton Photography / Photolibrary (b). 82 Corbis:
Danny Lehman (br). Dreamstime.com: Saurabh13 (b).
83 Corbis: airyuh / a.collectionRF / amanaimages (b);
Ocean (cr). Dreamstime.com: Lucaparodi (cl). 84
Getty Images: Matt Cardy. 85 Corbis: David Wrobel /
Visuals Unlimited (bc). 87 NASA: (cr). 89 Corbis: Galen
Rowell (t); Paul Souders (br). Dreamstime.com: Oleg
Kozlov (bl). 90-91 Getty Images: Slow Images /
Photographer's Choice (cr). 91 Dreamstime.com: Patrik
Kosmider (tl). Getty Images: Ron Erwin / All Canada
Photos (tr). 92 Corbis: Dave Reede / All Canada Photos
(b). 92-93 Getty Images: Carlos Davila / Photographers
Choice RF (bc). 94 Getty Images: Image Source (b).
95 Dreamstime.com: Mohamed Farhadi (b); Lester
(t). 96 Corbis: Michael S. Yamashita (br). 97 Dorling
Kindersley: Rough Guide (t). Dreamstime.com: Bin
Zhou (b). 98-99 Getty Images: Frank Krahmer / Peter
Arnold Images (c). 99 Getty Images: Fotosearch (tl); Wayne Lynch / All
Canada Photos (br). 100-101 Corbis: Frans Lanting.
102-103 Getty Images: Panoramic Images (b). 103
Dreamstime.com: Barefootfront (tr, tc); Debora Law
(tc); Melvinlee (cl). 104 Alamy Images: Stephen Frink
Collection (b). Dreamstime.com: Asther Lau Choon
Siew (c); David Espin (bl); Harmonia101 (bl). 105
Corbis: Martin Harvey (tr); Kevin Schafer (bl). Getty

Images: Saki Ono / Flickr Open (b). 106 Corbis:
Carlos Villoch / Robert Harding Specialist Stock. 107
Alamy Images: Jeff Mondragon (b). Getty Images:
Aaron Foster / Photographer's Choice (br). 108-109
Dreamstime.com: Vilainecrevette. 110 Alamy Images:
Clint Farlinger (br). Dreamstime.com: Nataq (bl).
David Woods (bl). 111 Corbis: Buddy Mays (cr); Neil
Rabinowitz (c). Dreamstime.com: John.59 (b). 112
Corbis: Michele Falzone / JAI (b). Getty Images:
Thomas Dressler / Gallo Images (tr). 113 Corbis:
Thomas Marent / Minden Pictures (c). Dreamstime.
com: Plotnikov (b). NASA: Visible Earth (cr). 114 Alamy
Images: Bill Bachman (cr). 115 Dreamstime.com:
Daria Angelova. 116-117 Corbis: George Steinmetz.
118 Corbis: Richard du Toit (br). Getty Images:
Visualization Studio Collection (bc). 120 NASA: (c, b).
Courtesy of the National Science Foundation: Reto
Boulton (cr). 121 Corbis: (bc). 122 Corbis: Imaginechina
(b); Frank Krahmer (tl). 123 Corbis: W. Perry Conway
(b). Getty Images: Don Johnston / All Canada Photos
(t). Dreamstime.com: Rudy Umans (b). 125 Corbis: Mark
Umans (bl). 125 Corbis: Mark Laricchia (tc).
Dreamstime.com: Ben Goode (tc/Cloud-to-Cloud)
Skydaver42 (tr); Intrepix (cr). Getty Images: SSODY
Images (t). 126 Getty Images: Graeme Norways /
Stone (b). 127 Corbis: Jim Oren van der Wal (t). 128-129
Corbis: Adam Jones / Visuals Unlimited (b). 128
Corbis: Tsui Hung / Redlink (b). 129 Corbis:
Momatiuk—Eastcott (br). 130-131 Corbis: Mike
Hollingshead / Science Faction. 132 Douglas P. Re
(c). Corbis: Jim Reed (br). 133 Corbis: Christopher
Morris (b); Mike Theiss / Ultimate Chase (t). 134
Dreamstime.com: Gordon Tipene (br). Getty Images:
STR / AFP (cr). NASA: Earth Observatory / Jeff
Schmaltz (tr). 135 Corbis: Andrew Brownbill / Epa.
136-137 Getty Images: Wiloughby Owen / Flickr.
Corbis: Paul Souders. 139 Dreamstime.com: Alexir (b).
Clc. 140-141 Corbis: Paul Souders (b). 141 Corbis:
Liu Liqun (b). Dreamstime.com: Ju Jayachandran (b).
142 Getty Images: John W Banagan / Stockbyte (b).
142-143 Dreamstime.com: Aecd Advertising and
Publishing (bc). 144 Corbis: David DuChemin / Design
Pics (b); Colin Monteath / Hedgehog House / Mind
Pictures (t). 145 Corbis: George Steinmetz.

Jacket images: Front: Dorling Kindersley: Chris
Reynolds and the BBC Team, cb, Andy Crawford /
Donks Models—modelmaker, cr, David Donkin—
modelmaker, ftr, cl, Donks Models—modelmaker, cr,
crb, Donk Models—modelmaker, tc, Simon Mumford,
cr. PunchStock: Corbis, cla; Back: Dorling
Kindersley: Donks Models—modelmaker, clb.
Spine: Dorling Kindersley: Simon Mumford, t.

All other images © Dorling Kindersley

For further information see: www.dkimages.com